Lanarkshire's MINING Legacy

In the hot, dusty atmosphere, miners needed to keep their mouths moist. Some sucked sweets or bits of coal while others chewed tobacco or drank water, but nothing could surpass cold tea, from a bent and battered tin flask.

Guthrie Hutton

Stenlake Publishing
1997

ISBN 1 84033 015 5

A continuous cable haulage system at Benhar Colliery.

INTRODUCTION

Glasgow and the old county of Lanarkshire were rich in coal. Early mines proliferated around the compact little city which should have had no problems with fuel supplies, but as industry developed, the price, controlled by a cartel of coal owners, began to rise. If Glasgow was to prosper the cartel had to be broken, but bad roads prevented alternative supplies from reaching the city. The solution was to cut a canal to the Monklands where good coal deposits were known to exist. The first length of canal was completed by James Watt (of steam engine fame) between 1770 and 1773. Ten years later it was extended and ten years later still, in 1793, it was completed from Calderbank to Port Dundas. The monopoly was broken and the great coal industry of Lanarkshire had begun.

By good fortune, the Monkland Canal was in the right place when the hot blast process of iron smelting was developed. Vast quantities of coal and ironstone were mined and moved around the rapidly expanding industry by barge. As railways developed the Monklands remained the iron making centre, while the new transport system encouraged the growth of iron and other industries elsewhere in the county. As iron gave way to steel the centre of Lanarkshire's mining industry moved south. Through the second half of the nineteenth century pit heads sprouted throughout the Motherwell, Wishaw and Hamilton areas. Lanarkshire coal was fuelling a huge industrial expansion, but unfettered development was accompanied by some terrible disasters; miners paid a high price in life and limb for the coal being burned in factories, houses, ships and railways at home and abroad.

By the end of the century the industry had reached its peak. In 1910, 220 of Scotland's 499 collieries were in Lanarkshire; 45,000 men worked underground with another 9,000 men and 1,200 women on the surface. Despite this dominance however, the coalfield was in decline, with more collieries closing than opening. The decline slowed during the First World War but accelerated between the Wars. By 1936 so many mines had closed in the Hamilton area that 300 men were travelling daily to the new Cardowan Colliery. A nervous County Council unsuccessfully sought Government assistance to rehouse the men in the Stepps area and asked mining companies to estimate the life of coalfields before they would build houses in other mining areas.

Even the Second World War, with its demands for all the coal the miners could dig, failed to halt the decline. By 1945 the Ministry of Fuel and Power regarded the county's industry as moribund with further decline as inevitable. A

Early 'cages' were no more than a platform with a frame attached to the winding cable and gave no protection to men like these about to descend.

fall in output of nearly 3 billion tons by the early 1950s was estimated by them, with a further 6.75 billion ten years later.

Nationalisation confirmed the trend. Pit closures in the three years to 1950 were expected to displace 6,000 men and proposals to dewater flooded pits were declared uneconomic by the new National Coal Board. Amidst accusations of anti-Lanarkshire bias, the Board concentrated developments in Fife, Ayrshire and the Lothians and a scheme to encourage Lanarkshire miners to emigrate to the new pits was introduced. Married men were guaranteed a house and, despite concerns that local people would resent them for jumping the housing queue, mining families began to drift away. A worried County Council was left with empty houses and no rents.

The Coal Board kept some uneconomic collieries working, to meet the needs of a Britain struggling to re-build after the war, but in the late 1950s demand was falling and by the end of the decade it was going down by 25 million tons a year. Developments in the steel industry boosted demand for coking coal from pits in the north of the county, but in other areas the decline continued. There were more ominous signs in the early 1960s as industry and railways turned to oil and smokeless zones reduced domestic use. In 1961, with fewer pits to manage, the Board merged its Central West and Central East administrative areas and as the Lanarkshire industry continued to shrink there were renewed calls for men to move to profitable pits in development areas.

In 1970 the county that once dominated the Scottish coal industry was down to its last four collieries. By the 1980s it was down to two. Closure of Cardowan in 1983 brought a proud industry and its long painful decline to an end.

Guthrie Hutton, 1997.

LANARKSHIRE INDUSTRY

HAULING ENGINE AT BOTTOM OF SHAFT   SCENE IN A LANARKSHIRE MINE Nº 6

The nineteenth century began with women and children hauling coal from the face to the pit head, but ended with steam driven underground haulage engines like this.

Underground, ponies did much of the haulage. This one has reached a junction where the U shaped end to the rails guided the hutches on and off a section of track – much easier than bends or complicated junctions.

Before blasting a section of coal, miners had to bore a pattern of deep holes for the explosive. The miner here is using a ratchet borer known as a rickety which is supported on a prop, set so that the pressure wedges it more firmly in place.

Coal deposits were worked by the sides of the Monkland Canal through the east end of Glasgow and into the Monklands area. Garthamlock Nos 5 and 6 pits were bought in 1906 by the Steel Company of Scotland whose Blochairn Steelworks were also beside the canal, a few miles to the west. The pits were used to supply the steel works, with any surplus output, including good household coal, being sold. Different seams were worked and abandoned at various times until about 1930.

Queenslie Colliery, to the south of the canal, was also operated by the Steel Company of Scotland, but, as well as using horse and cart, moved its coal by rail instead of canal. The bridge crossing the canal, beside Garthamlock Colliery above, carried a continuous haulage way from Queenslie to the Comedie screening plant to the north of Garthamlock. The screening plant was connected by a mineral railway across Cardowan Moss to the former Garnkirk and Glasgow Railway which was Glasgow's first public railway when it opened in 1831. It ran roughly parallel to the canal from Coatbridge to the city and competed directly for the Monklands coal trade.

The Comedie screening plant was also known as the Garthamlock Screens. It treated coal from Queenslie and Garthamlock, and also the output from Comedie Colliery which was situated to the east of Hogganfield Loch. Before going on the market, coal was graded and any stone that had come up from the pit was removed by hand. It was a hard job often done by women, but in this late 1920s picture of the picking tables at Comedie, it is being done by men.

West Maryston was a canalside mining village to the north of Baillieston which gloried in the unflattering nickname of 'the hole'. Moored to the offside bank, on the left, is a scow (a Scottish canal barge). At one time huge numbers of these scows carried coal and iron on the canal, but by the early twentieth century, when this picture was taken, only a few remained. This one is as likely to have been used for Sunday School outings as for moving coal.

Cold-blast furnaces were at work in the Monklands in the early years of the nineteenth century, but the scale of the industry was small. Around 1830 it was transformed when the hot blast process of iron smelting was developed and used with blackband ironstone. Although hot-blast used less coal, so many large works grew up in and around Coatbridge that, as a result, vast quantities of coal and ironstone were needed to keep them going. These Calder ironworks of William Dixon were among the first of the great works, along with William Baird's Gartsherrie works and others at Summerlee, Dundyvan and Langloan.

The pig iron produced at the great blast furnaces went to an assortment of malleable iron works which also needed coal. Within a few years the garden of Scotland had been turned into a noisy, smoke and fire filled 'no worse place out of hell'. Even the Monkland Canal steamed from the number of works using its water for cooling! This cradle of Scottish industry became the cradle of Scotland's railway system too when the first of a network of mineral railways, the Monkland and Kirkintilloch, opened in 1826. The prominent lattice girder bridge in the picture replaced the railway's original level crossing through the middle of Coatbridge.

Like many of the big iron masters, Robert Addie of Langloan ironworks, was also a coal owner. His company, Robert Addie & Sons Collieries Ltd, operated the Rosehall Collieries which ran to a number of sinkings on both sides of the River Calder, to the south of Coatbridge. When this picture of the 'Shawhead Pits' was taken in the early 1900s, Nos 3 and 14 were two of seven working shafts which, despite having individual names, were all part of Rosehall collieries. With the exception of the small Glen mine at Shawhead the Rosehall units had all closed before nationalisation with the last of the major sinkings, No. 10, closing in Feb. 1944. The Glen mine, which had been opened in 1940, closed in 1954.

Music has always been enjoyed in mining communities. At their height, when this picture of Rosehall Colliery Pipe Band was taken, the Rosehall pits employed over 1,500 people – more than any other in Lanarkshire. It was a sizeable pool of talent from which to recruit any number of bands, football teams and players in all the popular miners' recreations.

The Lanarkshire Coal Masters Association was slow to implement the Coal Mines Act of 1911 which required mine owners to provide trained rescue men at collieries, backed up by a central Mines Rescue Station. A station eventually opened at Ellis Street, Coatbridge in 1915 and received its first emergency call that November. A roof fall at Bedlay Colliery had cut three men off from the rest of the pit but before an air flow could be re-established one had been suffocated by the gas known as blackdamp. (The other dangerous pit gases are the explosive firedamp [methane] and the poisonous whitedamp [carbon monoxide] which is usually present in the cocktail of gases left after a fire or explosion).

Coatbridge became Scotland's only 'A scheme' Mines Rescue Station, permanently manned and equipped to attend incidents anywhere in Scotland, from Machrihanish on Kintyre to Brora in Sutherland. Part-time rescue teams for individual collieries were also trained there.

Three teams, of seven men and an instructor, provided round the clock cover. They trained regularly, with some sessions taken in a hot and humid atmosphere. There were replica mine workings under the building which could be

Mines Rescue teams were so well trained they were like an extra emergency service and able to assist at incidents like this tenement collapse in Shettleston.

filled with smoke by feeding the station fire with wet sawdust and diverting the flue. The men kept the station spotlessly clean and spent their days servicing safety equipment brought in from the pits. They and their families lived in station houses next door to the Regal Cinema – the children got free passes to the Saturday movies.

In the years that followed the setting up of the Coatbridge station there were many tragic accidents. Five men were entombed when a shaft collapsed at Neilsland Colliery, Hamilton, three died in a roof fall at Dykehead Colliery, Larkhall and gassings, explosions and runaway hutches killed and injured many more. Dreadful as such incidents were, one of the most harrowing disasters the early Coatbridge teams attended was at the McCracken Brothers' Stanrigg Colliery on the moors above Plains. On 9th of July 1918, about an acre of ground suddenly subsided into the Arbuckle pit, filling it with a peaty sludge. Nineteen men were trapped. They were only 66 feet below the mossy surface, but attempts to sink a shaft were hampered by the soggy ground, and gas foiled plans to drive a roadway from old workings. The unequal struggle was abandoned when bores into the highest section of the workings indicated nearly nine feet of water. Eight bodies were later recovered, but eleven remain in an unmarked grave threatened by encroaching open cast workings.

New regulations governing workings close to a boggy surface were issued following the inquiry into the disaster. They should have prevented a repetition, but in 1950 the Coatbridge brigade was called to Knockshinnoch Castle pit in Ayrshire where an enormous peat filled hollow, punctured by a heading, had drained into the pit. Thirteen died, but 116 trapped men were brought to safety, more than two days later, in one of the most dramatic mine rescues anywhere in the world.

The highly skilled men of the Rescue Brigades, honed by constant training, were ready for any challenge, even this rescue of a cow from an abandoned shaft on a Glenmavis farm. Using a temporary rig over the shaft one of the Coatbridge team is seen being lowered to attach a harness to the frightened animal. It was then hauled up and on reaching the surface gave its rescuer an unusual thank-you – a big lick on the face!

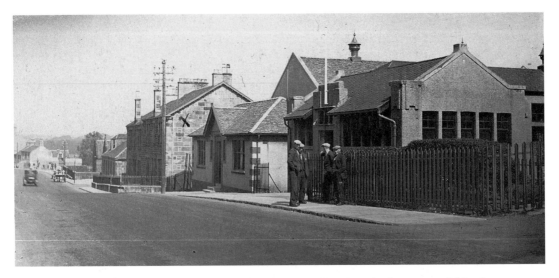

Chapelhall was a mining community long before the miners' institute in the centre of this picture was erected in the 1920s. The industry was revived by the NCB when they reopened a drift mine at nearby Gartness in 1949. It was called Knowhead but the miners dubbed it 'Nellie's mine' after the owner of the wee farm beside it. She gave the men soup, sandwiches and cups of tea and in return they let her take coal for her fire. They offered her some when the mine closed, but when they went to put it in the byre, they found it already well filled, the canny wee farmer had been hoarding coal for years.

Miners' Institute, Main Street, Longriggend

Under the Mining Industries Act of 1920 a fund was set up to provide facilities for the welfare of miners and mining communities. A penny was levied on every ton of coal to provide funds which were administered by a central Miner's Welfare Committee. Four fifths of the money had to be spent in the areas where it was raised and local committees determined what people in their area wanted. In Lanarkshire the preference was for recreation facilities and institutes like this one at Longriggend. A recreational facility (of sorts) was found in a small mine near Longriggend in the 1930s when a wisp of smoke led some carters to an illicit still.

Along from Plains, at Friar Brig, was the road which led to Ardenrigg mine. The mine was hidden in a fold of hills about 800 feet above sea level, just below where the Blackhill television transmitter mast was later built. In the severe winter of 1947 the buses could not get up the three mile road to the mine and these luckless miners were given the job of clearing it – and this is what the snow was like at the foot of the road! The coal had no such problems, it was brought by aerial ropeway across the moors to a railhead at the road end. In the background is Stepends brickworks which started making bricks from colliery waste in 1938.

In the early years the buses only went to Caldercruix and men had to walk over the moors past the Lily Loch to the Ardenrigg mines. The last mine, No. 6, was opened by the Ardenrigg Coal Company in 1926. It produced a high quality anthracitic coal from well ordered workings that belied these ramshackle corrugated-iron surface buildings. They were not improved by a botched wage robbery which blew down walls, but left the safe intact. The night shift men returning to the surface were shocked by the sight of police and wreckage, but they needn't have worried as they were paid in full! Like many workings Ardenrigg was plagued by rats. A new manager arrived and introduced an old solution – cats, eight at first, rising to about a dozen and they got rid of the menace. The mine closed in 1963.

Rich coal and ironstone deposits on the north side of the Clyde at Fullarton, Tollcross encouraged Thomas Edington and William Cadell to set up the Clyde ironworks in 1786. They were taken over by James Dunlop in 1810 and, six years later, his son Colin was in charge. He let James Beaumont Neilson use the works to perfect his hot blast technique for iron smelting. In 1930 the works were taken over by Colvilles Ltd and in 1970 by British Steel. They were closed soon after.

Late eighteenth century collieries in the Barrachnie area sent their coal to markets by the Monkland Canal and mining continued here at Barrachnie up to the early twentieth century. Pits either took the area name or coupled it with names like Barrachnie and Baillieston or Barrachnie and Springhill. A Springhill pit was working in the 1850s operated by a predecessor of the Mount Vernon Colliery Co., one of the big operators to the east of Glasgow. Many large companies worked Barrachnie coal including William Baird & Co. Ltd, the Bent Colliery Company and United Collieries.

Baillieston has a long history of mining from the canal age to the later railway age when the reserves to the south were exploited. The wet and narrow seams did not last long after the strikes of the 1920s and the bings, the physical evidence of a once big industry, quickly disappeared to provide bottoming for the old Glasgow to Edinburgh road. Miners housing has also now been replaced although it was fire that destroyed Society Row, soon after this photograph was taken in 1918.

The communal wash house, like this one outside Baillieston's Longlea Row, was a feature of miners' rows. It was shared between a number of houses and each housewife had a set day when it was her turn for the wash house. She washed the family's clothes first and when that chore was done she washed the children, each one taking their turn in the tub.

The Bredisholm Collieries were a group of very wet pits between Baillieston and Uddingston. The first Bredisholm pit was owned by a John Young who was taken over by the Glasgow Iron Company and finally by a large grouping of smaller companies known as United Collieries Ltd The last of the Bredisholm pits, Nos 3 and 4, to the north of the mining village of Aitkenhead, or Nackerty, closed in 1934 with the loss of 300 jobs.

Viewpark Colliery at Uddingston was a very modern pit when it was sunk by Robert Addie and Sons in the 1890s. Its two shafts, sixteen yards apart, were topped with impressive looking pitch pine headframes. The deep Viewpark workings were at risk from old, flooded workings and in 1934 Addie's paid the price of failing to agree a common pumping strategy with other mine owners. The prospect of imminent flooding forced them to close the workings from No. 1 shaft and although the colliery was kept going with new areas developed from No. 2, it did not last long and closure was announced in February 1942. The Minister of Mines, anxious to maintain coal production during the Second World War, stopped it being closed, but two weeks later the Lanarkshire Coal Production Committee accepted the inevitable.

About 7,000 men were being injured every year in Lanarkshire's pits and so in 1935 the Lanarkshire Orthopaedic Association opened out-patient clinics for them. They were set up in public health centres and miners' institutes across the county and their aim was to help men recover their fitness and return to work. They were the first such orthopaedic clinics in Britain.

The initiative was taken up on a national scale during the Second World War. The Ministry of Fuel and Power had to maintain production levels, but could not replace injured men easily and sought assistance from the Miner's Welfare Commission. In response, they opened a residential rehabilitation centre in 1943, at Gleneagles Hotel!

It proved so valuable that, when the War was coming to an end, alternative premises were sought and the Bellshill Road institute was taken over and adapted as a day centre. It was opened by the Chairman of the Miner's Welfare Commission in September 1945.

The Uddingston miners' institute, close to Viewpark in Bellshill Road, was opened in 1926.

Other rehabilitation centres were set up in England and Wales during and after the War, but despite plans for a residential centre at Aberdour in Fife, Uddingston remained the only one in Scotland. The Centre's surgeons, physiotherapists and social workers assessed the needs of every new case with the aim of returning injured men to a useful life. Those able to go back underground could test their fitness for the work in a model mine built by some of the early patients. Over 90% of men referred to the centre returned to colliery work.

The hall of the old institute was turned into a gymnasium and these outdoor gym facilities were set up too. They were also used by fully fit Mines Rescue Brigadesmen for physical training. The garden provided useful outdoor exercise and there were facilities for sports like football, handball, quoiting and bowling. Activities like archery, javelin throwing, trampolining and pillow fighting also became popular at the annual sports day.

Indoors, men could relax in the library or play chess, table tennis, darts, billiards or the piano. There was a carpentry workshop and some of the more seriously disabled men were trained to make a variety of saleable craft goods. At Christmas time the patients, like the hairy legged troupe of 'dying swans' in the lower picture, put on a revue – good for morale and recovery, if not for the macho image!

By the mid 1950s all of the other rehabilitation centres in Britain had been taken over by local Hospital Boards, but uniquely Uddingston's remained under the control of the Miner's Welfare Commission until it was taken over by the National Health Service in 1968. It is still used as a Medical Rehabilitation Centre.

opposite:

Carfin brickworks was supplied with coal and fireclay from three local pits connected to it by mineral railways. Like many brickworks it employed women, some of these are thought to be Lithuanian.

From the 1870s to the outbreak of the First World War, about a quarter of all Lithuanians were forced from their homes by financial hardship and political oppression. About 6,000 settled in Lanarkshire, particularly in and around Bellshill. For these oppressed rural people the prospect of a job and a company house were huge attractions even if the house was a hovel and the job underground. To begin with they were unpopular, because unwittingly, or driven by need, they took the jobs of striking Scottish miners. They were accused of being a danger to others because of language difficulties and of creating insanitary housing conditions with too many single men living together in tiny houses. Even their nationality was misunderstood – the locals called them Poles.

One of Scotland's pioneering ironworks was established at Omoa in 1787. Coal for it was mined on the spot and also brought by waggonway from other mines at Newarthill. Miners, with 'tally' lamps in their caps, are prominent in this group, in Omoa Square. There were about 180 houses in the square and by 1912 they were slums. The County Council sought to improve them and over a period of two years sent the bailiffs round early in the morning to evict the occupants. They piled people's furniture in the street before boarding up windows and doors. With nowhere to go one partially paralysed woman resorted to cooking breakfast for her four children over a fire in the road before finding somewhere else to stay. It is not known whether this picture was taken before or after the Omoa 'clearances'.

The fortunes of Bothwell Station and the neighbouring Bothwell Castle Nos 1 and 2 pits seem inextricably linked. The station opened in 1877, two years after the pits had been sunk by William Baird & Co. The pits closed in 1949 six years before the station's demise. As soon as the pits shut, water from the nearby Viewpark Colliery and the more distant Rosehall pits started to accumulate in the old workings, threatening to flood other pits south of the Clyde.

Shields Glen park, in the glen of the Whinny Burn, was once adorned by these attractive gardens and a backdrop of Shields Colliery – beauty and the bing perhaps! A number of pits were sunk, but when the colliery was acquired by the Glasgow Iron and Steel Company in 1894 only two undersized shafts were working. The company's principal target was the Splint coal for their Wishaw ironworks and a new 880 feet deep No. 9 shaft was sunk, in one year, to reach it. The adjacent No. 5 was also enlarged. Some seams were abandoned after the First World War and the rest of the colliery shut at the end of the Second. The nearby Parkhead Colliery operated a continuation of the Shields field below the Dalziell lands. It closed in 1928.

The Wishaw Coal Company's Dalzell pit was sunk to the Ell coal in 1869 and by 1900 had been enlarged and deepened to nearly 600 feet, or 100 fathoms (depths of pits [and oceans] are usually given in fathoms, six feet). The name was also changed to Dalzell and Broomside to differentiate it from another Dalzell pit. Much of the area worked was under the Clyde which meant it could be flooded if the roof strata collapsed. To prevent a disaster, a roof support system known as hydraulic stowage was introduced in 1910. Boiler ash and washer debris was mixed with water and the resultant sludge fed through holding pipes into areas cleared of coal. The sludge set hard and as well as supporting the roof, could be broken off in blocks and used to build 'pack' walls to contain more sludge. The lower seams were eventually flooded and when the upper seams were exhausted in 1948, the pit closed.

Hamilton Town Council looked into the possibility of using hydraulic stowage as a way of extracting the coal from under the town while avoiding subsidence. There were considerable deposits of coal under both it and Motherwell and many buildings were damaged, like these in Wellington Street, Motherwell. They could clearly have done with a bit of support, hydraulic or otherwise!

The Camp Colliery was on either side of the Muckle Burn close to the Camp railway viaduct over the Clyde. The pit suffered an explosion in 1861, a flood in 1876 and a pit-head fire in 1896. It was abandoned in November 1913. In this late nineteenth century picture, the man on the left of the cage at the pit bottom, has a peg leg. He could have been injured at the pit, but in these unforgiving days even a disabling injury, like the loss of a leg, would not stop a man from going to work. There was scant compensation and no safety net. If a man was not working he got no pay, he and his family could starve and would be evicted from their company house.

Men risked injury all the time in narrow seams, but not all were as thin as this. The most prized household coal throughout area, the Ell, was named after an old Scots unit of measure about a yard long. The ell was not standardised, and the thickness of the coal named after it varied too, ranging, in places, from less than one to over two ells thick. Other seams had names like Main, Pyotshaw, Virtuewell, Splint, Humph, Kiltongue and Drumgray.

Men working on their side at a narrow seam like this often kept themselves off the pavement with a 'shoulder board', a piece of wood about twelve inches by six inches raised at one end by a one inch block.

Lanarkshire's mines were almost invariably 'fiery' or gassy and the man here, a fireman or oversman, is using a lamp to test for gas. Two inventors, Sir Humphrey Davy and George Stephenson both produced safety lamps in 1815 although subsequent developments of flame safety lamps were often just called 'Davy Lamps'. Perverse as ever, Scottish miners called theirs 'Glennie' lamps, probably a corruption of another safety lamp inventor, Dr. Clanny, whose lamp was the first to replace Davy's wire gauze with a glass cylinder. It was the real forerunner of subsequent safety lamps which were adapted, as here, to test for gas. An experienced fireman could tell from the height of the flame what percentage of gas was present.

The original Newcastle Davy Lamp and subsequent development.

The Clanny Lamp.

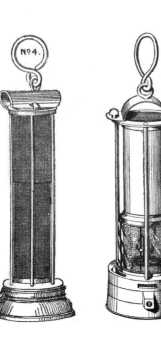

Only 1.5% of British coal was mined by machine in 1899 when Alexander Anderson, Thomas Boyes and Daniel Burns, set up in business as Anderson Boyes, at Flemington, Motherwell. Their aim was to produce coal cutting and other underground electrical plant and to equip collieries with plant from the power house to the coal face. They sold the first disc cutter to the Summerlee Iron Company and, responding to American attempts to break into British markets, developed their first chain cutter in 1906. Miners were fearful of losing their jobs and initially resistant to machinery. As the First World War approached, however, the company's cutters and conveyors were at work in many collieries, contributing to an output in Scotland that was 12.5% higher than the UK average.

Despite having to make munitions during the war the company continued to develop new cutters and by the mid 1920s nearly 50% of Scottish coal was cut by machine. The arcwall machine, regarded as a great advance in 1924, was superseded nine years later by a yet more versatile machine. During the Second World War, while again working on munitions, the company collaborated with other manufacturers to produce the AB Meco-Moore cutter loader, the forerunner of modern power loading shearers. At its height the Flemington works employed 1,250 people, but as mining contracted in Britain the company went through a number of amalgamations and reductions. It diversified into world wide markets, but in July 1997, two years short of its centenary, its closure was announced, ending one of the county's last links with the mining industry.

The road running between these Clydesdale Rows is now Carbarns Road and the picture looks south from what is now Netherton Road. The road continued beyond the rows to the Clydesdale, Carbarns and Muirhouse Collieries where many of the occupants of the rows will have worked. Clydesdale Colliery was abandoned in 1903. Running water was a rarity for such communities as indicated by the communal pump outside the houses on the left.

The Coltness Iron Company operated an ironstone mine at Branchal before the First World War, but closed it in 1913. It was reopened as a coal mine in 1924, but experienced problems during the Second World War which caused the Company to look for alternative sites. It survived into nationalisation, but after a few difficult years the Coal Board closed it in July 1959 as uneconomic.

Miners Institute, Overtown

Finlayson Photo

Overtown and Waterloo Miners' institute was opened in April 1924 when W. H. Telfer, managing director of the Coltness Iron Company, turned a silver key to unlock the door. Inside was a hall which seated 500 people, projection box, cloakrooms, kitchen, billiard room, carpet bowls room, reading room and private baths and spray. It had electric light throughout and a concert was held in the evening to inaugurate the new facility.

Getting to and from the coal could be as hard as digging it. These men at Overtown are climbing an incline, assisted by a 'Telpher' – a continuous overhead man haulage system that may have helped the legs, but was hell on the arms. Overtown was an all electric pit begun in 1928 by the Coltness Iron Company. It reached peak output in the late 1930s, but by the time of nationalisation the company had it earmarked for closure. The Coal Board struggled with geological difficulties until December 1953 when bores were put down to see if continued drivage was possible, but with water also a problem the pit closed the following June. It was dismantled and the shafts filled in. Two years later plans were being laid to dewater the pit, dig the shafts out again and deepen them to reach seams of coking coal. The revived pit lasted until 1968.

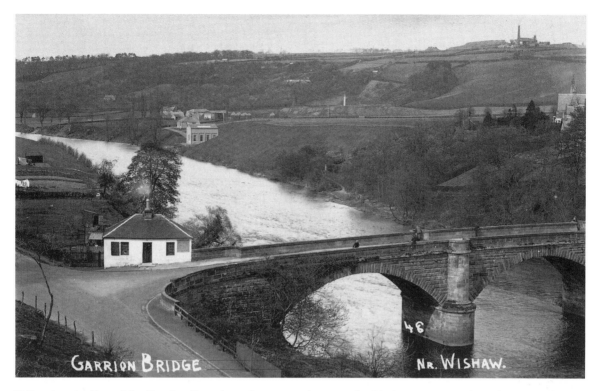

Following the line of the Garrion Burn from Overtown down to the Clyde, were a number of mines called Garriongill operated by the Coltness Iron Company. Nos 10 and 11 mines can be seen stretching from Garrionhaugh Farm to the church on the right in this view looking north across Garrion Bridge. On the hill, to the right, is what appears to be Garriongill Nos 1 and 12.

Henry Houldsworth was already well established in the cotton industry in Manchester and Glasgow when he bought the Coltness Estate, with its estimated reserves of 36 million tons of coal and 2 million tons of ironstone. He set up the Coltness Iron Company at Newmains, then a small village on the Ayr to Edinburgh road. The single blast furnace was tapped for the first time in May 1839, but the infant works had to contend with poor transport links until the railway arrived in the 1840s. Over the years, six more blast furnaces were added and in the late nineteenth century the company moved into high quality carbon steel production. A brick works, briquetting works, fireclay works and a works to make cement with granulated slag were all set up. From Newmains the Company expanded to take over collieries in England as well as taking a controlling interest in other Lanarkshire mining companies.

This picture postcard of a miner's row, was sent from Morningside, Newmains, but its actual location is not known. The houses have clearly suffered from undermining with repointed brickwork, sagging roofs and broken lintels. They are typical single ends, two to a block, with rain water butts and an open sheugh (drain). Inside such houses, flooring was often just beaten earth or slate, walls were unplastered and attempts to make them better by applying wallpaper with a flour and water paste, simply provided food for bugs and vermin. Communal ash pits with overflowing outside toilets were the norm.

Paradoxically, one Lanarkshire mine manager would have taken a dim view of the bare-footed children. A hard man, intolerant of any employee not prepared to work long shifts in dirty, wet and dangerous conditions, he nevertheless hated to see unshod children and kept a range of child sized boots in the house for them.

The Coltness Iron Company's Kingshill No. 1 pit at Allanton, seen here about 1950, went into production in 1919 to work a three mile wide field of coking coal that stretched five miles towards Forth. At the time of nationalisation the workings had reached two and a half miles from the pit bottom and underground haulage systems were extended to the limit. Further development was physically and financially impossible, but the pit got a new lease of life in 1952 with the opening of Kingshill No. 3 and the installation of a new treatment plant.

Pit head baths were set up at Kingshill No. 1 out of Coltness funds, instead of waiting for money from the Welfare Fund. Seated with his hat on his knee, in the centre of this group at their opening in June 1929, is Managing Director, W.H. Telfer. He was noted for his enlightened attitude to miners' welfare and is thought to have built the first pit head baths in Scotland, at Douglas Castle, when he was General Manager of Wilson's and Clyde Coal Co., a company that had close links with Coltness. He was very much a company man, born in Overtown and receiving his early education in the company school there.

Before this new treatment plant was installed at Kingshill No. 1, the output of the local Coltness pits was treated at the Royal George washer at Newmains. It was superseded by the Kingshill plant which also treated coal from Branchal and Overtown. In May 1968 manpower at Kingshill No. 1 was reduced by 25%, but the savings were insufficient to save the pit from closure although the washer remained operational to treat output from Kingshill No. 3. The massive bing, which grew to dominate Allanton, has now been landscaped and planted as a community woodland.

Allanton grew following the development of Kingshill No. 1. The County Council, in equal partnership with Coltness Iron Company, built a village of 250 houses set back from the Edinburgh Road. Although mining is now a thing of the past, street names like Houldsworth Crescent, Coltness Avenue and Kingshill Road still reflect the village origins.

The Second World War forced the Coltness Iron Company to postpone plans to sink a new shaft to where the No. 1 faces had reached underground, but in August 1946 sinking of Kingshill No. 3 began. The NCB speeded up the work to meet the growing demand for coking coal. The new fifteen foot diameter concrete lined shaft went down over 750 feet to where level roadways were driven to intercept the coal. A loading chute, connected by conveyor to the working faces, delivered the coal to 2.5 ton mine cars which were hauled to the pit bottom by diesel locomotives. Kingshill No. 3 was the first major NCB development in Scotland to be brought into production in the spring of 1952. The predicted life for the Kingshill units was 30 years, but by 1969, No. 3 was set to close although it was kept going on a month to month basis for another five years.

The Coconut Well, a moorland spring of natural mineral water, was a favourite picnic site for Allanton folk until Kingshill No. 3 was built around it. Miners threw loose change into the twenty foot deep well and, when the pit closed, one of them, Arthur 'Monkey' Wilson, donned his diving gear and retrieved the money for his favourite charity. A forest now cloaks the colliery site and a bottling plant has been set up amongst the pit head ruins to market spring water from the 'forest glade'.

This two and a half mile long continuous haulage way was built across the moors to get the mine cars of coal from Kingshill No. 3 to the new treatment plant at Kingshill No. 1.

The big boys of the NCB regarded private mines with disdain – 'mucky holes with small roads', but they did do one thing right – they made money! Blackhall mine at Allanton was operated by the Blackhall Mining Company to work the Armadale Main coal with seventeen miners and three surface workers.

The entrances to drift mines like these, and the NCB's posher versions, were known as 'in gaun e'es' (in going eyes).

The Catcraig Coal Company of Motherwell operated this Catcraig mine at Braidwood with only eight miners and two men on the surface working a seam of household coal.

Robert Currie opened his first mine at Larkhall in 1941 to supply his Carluke coal merchant's business with its own coal. It was followed by this Gillfoot mine at Braidwood, which was operated under the name of Gillfoot Coal Company. It was opened in 1957 and continued in production with twenty seven miners and nine surface men until 1970.

The Shotts Iron Company was set up in 1801. It prospered through the Napoleonic wars and a second blast furnace was built. Hot blasting was adopted in 1832, a third furnace was built in 1840 and the arrival of the railway in 1846 gave the works a further boost. Expansion continued through the rest of the nineteenth century and two more furnaces were added along with brickworks, briquetting works and coking plant. The minerals in the surrounding area were extensively worked and pits in other parts of Lanarkshire and the Lothians were developed. The works struggled through the 1920s and 30s and even kept some furnace activity going through the Second World War, but with most of its assets nationalised, and only the ageing blast furnaces left, the company called it a day in 1947.

The miners' institute in Dyfrig Street, Dykehead was bigger and better than most being built on two floors at a cost of £11,000 of which almost £2,000 was raised locally to supplement the Welfare Fund grant. The institute was opened in October 1924 by Matthew Brown, managing director of Shotts Iron Company. It had a hall, rooms for billiards and carpet bowls and two rooms set aside for photography. The library and reading room had 1,300 books gifted by Lanarkshire Education authority and there were also a swimming pool, sprays, foot and 'slipper' baths.

Stane Colliery, sunk in 1897, was one of three Kepplehill Coal Company pits taken over by Shotts Iron Company in 1918. It was closed briefly in the 1920s as part of a scheme to preserve capacity in the industry. In the run up to nationalisation the Ministry of Fuel and Power warned it, and some other old pits, to stop unofficial strikes and increase output or they would close. Despite raising output by 8% it was reprieved only half an hour before the deadline in October 1946. When it did close, in December 1955, it was the sixth Shotts pit to be shut down since nationalisation. Its closure was preceded by the NCB's drift mine at Stane which was shut down in 1953, with the loss of 100 jobs, after less than five years in operation.

In the post war 1950s, while the coal industry was adjusting to the new order and society was coming to terms with the cold war, the abandoned Stane Colliery was taken over for this Civil Defence exercise.

This engine at Stane could have been used, either for driving a ventilation fan or the underground haulage systems. Cables from surface mounted haulage engines were taken down the pit shaft to an underground drive shaft which transferred the power to the haulage roads. The Shotts Iron Company made such engines and equipped its own pits like Rimmon and Calderhead with them.

A connecting road allowed the adjacent Calderhead and Rimmon pits to operate as one. They worked seams that were the same as those at the lower levels around Motherwell and Hamilton, the upper strata having been denuded in the geological past. Closure notices were issued to men in the surviving Calderhead Nos 3 and 4 in 1946 and, although they were withdrawn, the pit faced an uncertain future until the NCB took over. Despite being reorganised it was always teetering on the brink and in 1958, with the output down to 150 tons a day, it became the seventh pit in the Shotts area to close. Two years later the pit head buildings were renovated as this training centre for apprentice tradesmen for the Central East Area, but Shotts suffered further blows when the NCB decided to close its waggon building shop and, in 1969, its central workshops.

When horses came to the surface, like this one at Southfield, their eyes were covered to protect them from the glare. They only came up when the miners were on holiday or on a prolonged strike – not uncommon around Shotts! The Company's reputation for harshness was matched by their miners' militancy. Southfield men supported the 'communist led' breakaway union, the United Mineworkers of Scotland, in the period of inter-union rivalry following the 1926 lock-out and strike. Like Stane and Calderhead, Southfield was warned in 1946 to increase production or face closure. Production leaped by 12.5%, but the pit only survived until 1959 when it became the eighth Shotts unit to close since the NCB take-over. Northfield was the ninth and last Shotts pit to close in July 1961.

The miners in the Coltness Iron Company's Dewshill pit worked an anthracitic coal in very wet and unpleasant conditions. The pit was remodelled in 1923, but by the 1940s was experiencing serious problems. In 1943 the Ministry of Fuel and Power decided it would have to close so that work could be concentrated on pits with a higher output. The Union wanted a maintenance team retained, to save the pit for post war development, but despite a year long argument the pit was closed. Duntilland mine was sunk in the same area to work the Upper Drumgray coals when Dewshill closed, but thin seams, bad roof conditions and water led to its closure in 1951.

Coltness Iron Company opened Hassockrigg pit, with its dramatic twin headframes, in 1885. It worked thin seams of steam and household coal and, like Dewshill, was redeveloped in the 1920s to open out the lower coals. Little publicity surrounded its closure, because the announcement coincided with that for the closure of two of the NCBs showpiece developments, Glenochil in Clackmannanshire and Rothes in Fife. Partial shut down in February 1962 was followed by complete closure in July.

With a lack of proper wash houses at West Benhar rows, near Harthill, women would heat water outside, in large iron pots like the one standing on the open hearth on the left and scrub the clothes in the wooden tubs. Most of the miners' rows had no bathing facilities and the men washed in a tub in front of the kitchen range. The sheugh, the open gutter running through the middle of the picture, was the only means of drainage.

Muirhead pit at West Benhar was closed in 1921 but the flooded pit got a new lease of life in 1936 when the Summerlee Iron Company took it over. They de-watered it, brought it back into production and kept it going until the NCB moved in. When it closed in October 1962, with the loss of 480 jobs, it was the end of mining in the Harthill area, but not the end of coal getting. Opencast operations (they can't really be called mining!) have won large amounts of coal from the moorland south of Eastfield up to Peden's Stone. Some of this coal was not far below the surface and up to twelve feet thick.

Some Harthill coal was mined very near the surface, like the private mine which filled with turnips after a shot firing and these old workings exposed by an early opencast. This mine has been worked by 'stoop and room', a method in which miners work to a boundary taking out 'rooms' of coal around columns of coal called 'stoops', which are left to support the roof. When the boundary is reached the miners retreat to the entrance removing the stoops and allowing the roof to collapse behind them. These old workings have not been 'stooped out', perhaps because they were so close to the surface.

The other, more common, technique in Scotland was longwall advancing. Parallel roadways were driven, a set distance of about two hundred yards apart, and the coal taken out between them on a long face. This miner appears to be advancing into the coal from a roadhead. He is using an electric drill to prepare shot holes instead of the ratchet rickety of the early miners. The props or 'trees' have been beautifully set at the regulation three feet apart. Timber props that oozed sap when they were knocked into place were preferred by miners for their load bearing qualities.

To get coal from the face to the haulage road it was either shovelled into hutches, or on to a conveyor. In this narrow seam the miner is loading the bottom of a conveyor belt; the top of it is above his shovel. At the road the coal was ploughed off the belt before it fouled up the mechanism. Miners 'graded' each other by the size of the shovel they could wield, a 'No. 10 shovel' was held in awe by his colleagues.

Ponies were part of the mining community, they lived in underground stables and were fed and cleaned by their handlers after the day's work. They knew when it was time for a break and pestered men for food. If it was slow in coming they stole it, by lifting miners' piece tins in their mouths and dropping them on the pavement to open them. Some could even lift these metal flasks and take a drink, without needing the kind of help being given here.

The miners in this group of pictures, thought to be from Benhar about 1950, are all wearing American made canvas caps fitted with a compressed cardboard bracket to hold a carbide lamp. It had containers of calcium carbide and water which, when mixed, gave off the gas ethyne or acetylene which burned with a bright flame. The carbide lamp replaced the tallow ('tally') lamp which miners simply hooked on to a cloth cap. Its reservoir was filled with animal fat or seal oil and the wick, led through a funnel, burned with a smoky flame. Battery lamps and helmets were introduced around 1940, although both seemed to take a while to reach Benhar!

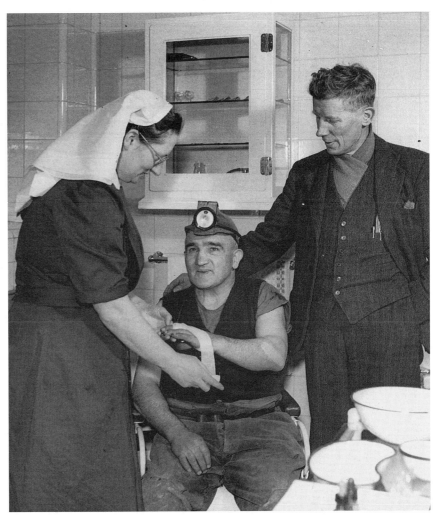

Baths were opened in 1950 at Benhar with the main medical centre for the NCB's Central East area attached to them. It employed a full time nurse who is seen here attending to a contractor's injured finger, while a sympathetic pit manager looks on – 'there, there lad'!

Kingshill No. 2, unofficially known as Queenshill, was begun in 1928. It was some distance from Kingshill No. 1, but was eventually connected to it underground. The 900 foot shaft almost went back down to sea level from a pithead 925 feet up. The Coltness Iron Company believed it was the highest in the country although the Beoch mines in Ayrshire were over 1,000 feet above sea level and the lead mines at Wanlockhead higher, but they were mines! An unsuccessful attempt to stave off closure, by reducing the work force to concentrate on the most economic work, failed to stop the pit being shut in 1963.

Andrew Robb of Forth enjoyed the typical miners' leisure pursuits. He bred and raced dogs, was a quoiter and a good footballer, playing in goal for Haywood Wanderers and Forth Wanderers. He was over six foot tall, big for a miner (and a goalie!) although, when he started helping his father at the coal face of William Dixon's Wilsontown pit, he was a wee boy of twelve. It was 1891, wireless telegraphy was in its infancy and Britain was expanding its Empire in Africa. Seventy years later, Africa was being decolonised, a space man was orbiting the earth and the National Coal Board was compelling a reluctant eighty two year old Andrew to retire. He was pit bottomer on the night shift at Kingshill No. 2 and the oldest working miner in Scotland. He is seen here, on the left, at Allanton Miners' Institute with Kingshill Group Manager Arthur McAlpine who presented him with an inscribed barometer and a wallet with £100 pounds. He would have preferred to have been given his job back!

John and William Wilson of Cleugh House, Forkens were partners in a successful London business when their elder brother Robert persuaded them to extend the family estate. The new land contained ironstone which encouraged the brothers to set up Lanarkshire's first coke fired ironworks in 1779. Despite inexperience and the remote moorland location, the works prospered and the name of Forkens was changed to Wilsontown. A second blast furnace, forge and rolling mill were added but, despite the excellence of the plant and the quality of its product, all was not well. John and William, concerned about Robert's mismanagement, bought out his share in 1785, but, spilt between their London and Scottish interests the two began to quarrel. Distrust gave way to acrimony, litigation and eventually, in 1812, to bankruptcy. Nine years later the works were bought by William Dixon for a fraction of their former value, but they were never in sustained production again and closed in 1842. In the early twentieth century there were still substantial remains. This viaduct carried the waggon road that brought minerals to the works, and fed the furnaces and engines built into the steep sides of the Mouse Burn. The counting house and weigh-house were built on the culvert in the foreground (the 'cundie' to local youngsters).

The Wilsons brought experienced ironworkers, miners and trades people to Wilsontown. They all had to be housed and, by the time the enterprise collapsed, 450 houses, like these in Quality Row, had been built.

Like other industrial concerns of the time the Wilsontown ironworks had its own company store. It supplied a wide variety of goods from clothing and footwear to food and household utensils. Employees had no alternative but to use the store, even in death there was no escape – it sold coffins too! It sold beer, but not whisky although the ironworkers and miners were probably unconcerned because an illicit still operated in the area until its discovery in 1812. A new supply was soon established. The Wilsons prevented the trustees of the New Lanark to Wilsontown turnpike road from erecting a toll bar at

Wilsontown. They were concerned about the cost of tolls on materials going in and out of the works, but when the works failed, the road trustees erected a toll bar and this toll house. The house was licensed to sell drink which the licensee, disregarding legal restrictions, did at any time of the day or night, much to the chagrin of Dixon's store!

Pleasance Row was at the entrance to Dixon's Wilsontown pit.

After the collapse of iron working, mining was Wilsontown's main industry, but it remained small scale until the arrival of the railway in 1860. As the lines extended, mining expanded to Climpy and Haywood. Dixon's worked the Main coal around Wilsontown and leased the gas coal to a partnership who cleared out the Holmsyke Level. It was a remarkable 2.75 mile long drain, built by the Wilsons to keep their mines clear of water. When the lease ran out in 1885 it allowed Dixon's to develop the coalfield. They sunk the large Wilsontown pit in 1898.

There was a ready market for Wilsontown coal and its high quality metallurgical coke was still being used by the iron and steel industry, more than a hundred years after the ironworks failed. The coke ovens, seen here on the right, were always warm and in the winter, homeless men gravitated to the area. They lived in a small colony near Dixon's pit and at night got a wee heat next to the coke ovens.

This old engine, photographed before it was dismantled, was made at William Dixon's Govan ironworks – the famous Dixon's Blazes.

Wilsontown pit broke the 1926 strike early and unprintable descriptions of the men involved are still spoken around Forth today.

The pit itself was closed through exhaustion in February 1955. It was not however the end of mining in the area because private mines like Abbey, Backshot and more recently Rashiehill have continued working the Wilsontown Main coal. The Mansefield Hotel's Colliery Restaurant celebrates the area's mining connections with themed decor and a working model of a pit.

The gas coal at Haywood, to the east of Wilsontown, was first worked by the Coltness Iron Company in 1862 and later by the Haywood Gas Coal Company. At one time Haywood had a population of 1,400 people, but although there is little left of the village, its place in mining history is assured. It was here, in December 1922, that the first miners' institute in Britain, built under the Miner's Welfare Scheme, was opened. It was a simple corrugated iron building with asbestos slate roof. Inside was a wood lined hall, retiring rooms and toilets, but within a few years of its opening the Haywood pits had closed.

Haywood Wanderers carved out their place in local history too. They were an intimidating outfit, unbeaten at home in fourteen years and regarded with local pride as 'the dirtiest team in Scotland'.

Tarbrax is just inside the border with West Lothian and its shale oil industry is more usually associated with that county. The industry was inspired by one of Scotland's great unsung industrial pioneers James 'Paraffin' Young who patented his oil distillation process in 1850 and built one of the first refineries in the world, at Bathgate. He started extracting oil from cannel coal, or torbanite, but the limited supply was expensive so he adapted to using oil shale. When his patent expired others jumped on the bandwaggon and oil works spread across the county and into Lanarkshire at Tarbrax. The industry made Young a very wealthy man and he used some of his considerable fortune to help fund the missionary work of one of Lanarkshire's better known sons, David Livingstone.

The Tarbrax oil works and candle factory were owned in turn by the Lanark Oil Co., the Caledonian Mineral Oil Co. and the Tarbrax Oil Company who took over in 1904, sunk new mines and built this new works. They were taken over by the Pumpherston Oil Company in 1912 which was absorbed five years later by Scottish Oils Ltd, a subsidiary of the Anglo Persian Oil Co., which later became B.P. In the 1920s, with the price of shale oil rising and a world glut of crude, the industry contracted rapidly and the Tarbrax works closed.

Coal for the oil works was mined at nearby Woolfords which was the unlikely scene of a riot during the first national miners' strike in 1912. About 700 men broke in to Woolfords No. 5 pit after throwing bricks and stones at it. They threw weights down the shaft to damage the cage and set fire to the headframe and engine house.

Houses in Crosswood Terrace, Tarbrax, which still bear their company village number, are seen here behind the narrow village bowling green and now disused tennis courts.

Govan Colliery stretched along the south side of the Clyde and into the western edge of Rutherglen Parish with its Nos 5 and 6 pits. This view of No. 5 pit from the West, or 'Jenny's', Burn probably dates from the late nineteenth century. The miners are wearing 'tally' lamps in their caps indicating an early date before the dangers of naked flames were fully understood. The pit was sunk around 1860 on the site of the old Toryglen Pit and worked to the 1920s. Govan Colliery was managed in the late eighteenth century by Tynesider, William Dixon, who, with his son William, went on to own the colliery and establish one of the major Lanarkshire coal and iron companies. The older Govan pits were connected by a wooden railed mineral railway, but the trucks beside No. 5 pit here, are on metals linked to the adjacent Polmadie Mineral Depot and the main Glasgow to London railway.

One of the pits that made the 'wee roun lums o' Ru'glen' reek so briskly was Farme Colliery near Dalmarnock Bridge. It was famous for this atmospheric condensing steam engine, which was erected in 1809 and wound about 3 million tons to the surface, before the pit closed about 1916. Longevity at Farme was not confined to engines, because in 1911 the manager, James Anderson, whose family had been in mining since 1620, celebrated fifty years in the job. He claimed that if all the roadways made in his time were joined together they would have made 35 Channel tunnels. Rutherglen encapsulated the Lanarkshire problem, with over twenty feet of rich coal in seams close to the surface but, by the First World War, it was gone, mined to exhaustion.

They had been digging coal in Cambuslang for centuries too before the Kirkhill, or Toll, pit on the right, was sunk around 1875. It was at the junction of Hamilton and Croft Roads and numerous old workings had to be stabilised during its development. They caused flooding in later years too. The Kirkhill workings went into the abandoned Village pit at Cambuslang Cross, where iron tipped wooden picks and shovels were found along with an old creel, a relic of the days when women carried coal out of pits on their backs. Despite producing an excellent house coal, much sought after by the Glasgow coal hawkers, the Toll pit closed in 1904. Gateside, which closed in 1946, and Coats Park, which shut in 1958, were the last working pits in the area.

At the end of these rows beyond the village school was No. 1 pit of Newton Colliery. It was sunk in the early 1850s, joined by a second shaft in 1874 and connected to the Hallside pit by 1888. No. 1 outlasted the others, was renamed Blantyreferme No. 3 and was one of the oldest pits in Scotland when it closed in 1964. Closure was forced on the NCB when it was discovered that water from the abandoned Gateside Colliery at Cambuslang was not reaching the pumps at Priory pit (Bothwell Castle Nos 3 and 4). The probability of it building up in old uncharted workings, posed an unacceptably high risk to Newton.

A short walk across the fields to the east of Newton is the steep valley of the Rotten Calder, seen here at its confluence with the Clyde. In the distance is Haughhead Colliery. It was a very wet pit, opened by the Haughhead Coal Co. and later taken over by the Mount Vernon Colliery Co. The site of the old pit is now a golf driving range which still suffers from subsidence.

Close to Haughhead was the Blantyreferme colliery sunk by the Ayrshire company, A & G Moore, in 1894. Caldervale, its associated pit village close to the Rotten Calder, was so well hidden from the road it was known locally as 'Fin-me-oot'. In the 1950s the NCB added to the Blantyreferme complex by building a brickworks close to 'Fin-me-oot'. This new mine was driven to dig a rich red clay. It did not last long and the parent colliery was closed in 1962.

Bardykes Colliery near Blantyre was on the site of an old infectious diseases hospital which gave it the alternative name of Spittal pit. It was sunk, with some difficulty, through water bearing sandstone between 1874 and 1877. It reached a depth of about 1350 feet and worked the minerals under three adjoining estates. After less than thirty years it was shut down and dismantled after a dispute over royalties between the proprietors and the operators, Merry and Cunninghame. Six hundred miners lost their jobs, but not for long, because the Summerlee Iron Company took over the abandoned colliery and, after an eighteen month refit, reopened it in 1908. Haulage and other machinery was electrically driven and only the winding engines remained powered by steam.

At the time of its reopening the pit was expected to last for another thirty years, but it kept going for longer than that. It could have closed in 1949, when No. 2 shaft caved in, but although it was out of action for a year while a new road was driven from Newton, it reopened and worked until 1962. The picture shows the remaining No. 1 shaft; No. 2 shaft was on the left where the ramp can be seen. In the distance, between headframe and chimney, is the Priory Colliery bing.

Priory Colliery, on the western edge of Blantyre, was officially known as Bothwell Castle Nos 3 and 4 even though the parent colliery, Bothwell Castle Nos 1 and 2, was on the other side of the Clyde. Flooded after closure, the No. 1 and 2 workings posed a threat to the Priory workings which were shut in 1951 as a precaution. A 7,000 name petition was raised in Blantyre to save the pit, but the Coal Board wanted to use it as a pumping station to save Newton, Bardykes and Blantyreferme from being flooded. After months of discussion, the Union agreed to the Board's plans but persuaded them to continue working the upper coal. The pit finally closed in 1959 but remained as a pumping station.

Priory Colliery, seen here at the end of its life, was sunk by William Baird & Company in 1889. Bardykes, Newton, Blantyreferme and Priory Collieries all became linked by an extensive network of underground passages.

A TYPICAL MINING FAMILY

Dressed in their Sunday best for this picture from around 1900, the McGuigan's, of the Bardykes, or 'Spittal', Rows were a typical mining family. Mr McGuigan was Irish, one of many, like the later Lithuanians, who escaped poverty in their native land to work in Scottish pits. Mrs McGuigan came from a more prosperous Glasgow family who disowned her when she married a miner, no doubt regaling her with sentiments like:

> The day ye marry a collier chiel,
> That's the day ye'll ne'er do weel,
> A gie wee poke will haud yer meal,
> The day ye marry a collier.

But she bore ten children, eight survived and because they all worked in the pits, the family enjoyed a tolerable level of security. The baby, the wee boy in the foreground, left the pits through ill health and became active in the Communist Party. He helped to raise funds for the Republican cause in the Spanish Civil War. The two girls on the left both worked at the picking tables. The boy next to them was a 'tramp brusher'. Brushers, or 'reddsmen', did the dangerous work of clearing loose rock from the workings and roadways to keep them safe for others. Tramps were not tied to a single pit, but moved around looking for the best paid work, getting paid by the day, 'on the shovel'. His brother, to the right, started in the pits but, like the baby, was forced out through ill health made worse by working in wet conditions. The eldest son's mining career was brought to a premature end by nystagmus or, 'Glennie blink', an eye disorder that led to blindness for many miners. It was caused by working in the dim light of flame safety lamps. The younger brother on the right became a fireman and rescue brigadesman at Bardykes. He earned a commendation for an improvised rescue which saved a man, whose back had been broken in a roof fall, from further paralysing injury. The wee girl on the right, like her sisters, worked at the picking tables from the day she left school to the day she married. An earlier generation of her husband's extended family had lost six men in the infamous Blantyre disaster. Just another typical mining family!

THE BLANTYRE DISASTER

The explosion was heard, all the women and children,
With pale anxious faces made haste to the mine,
When the truth was made known, the hills rang with their mourning,
Two hundred and ten young miners were slain.

On 22nd October 1877 an explosion lasting several minutes ripped through the Splint coal workings of Nos 2 and 3 pits of William Dixon's Blantyre Colliery. The No. 3 head frame was wrecked by a roaring column of flame, coal dust and debris and the blast also disabled No. 2 shaft. Twenty three men were later brought out of No. 2 alive; no-one survived in the No. 3 workings. Over two hundred died in Scotland's worst mining disaster.

When the lethal gases were cleared the awful destruction was revealed. The blast appeared most violent in an area of No. 2 pit, but because explosions travel against the air current, the worst effects were in the No. 3 workings. There were mutilated bodies, props blown over, trap doors and bratticing shattered, rails and sleepers torn up. Some places were piled high with mashed debris, others swept clean.

The true cause was never established. A spark or naked light were thought to have ignited some gas, but ventilation almost certainly contributed. The air current was created by a furnace at the base of No. 5 shaft, about thirty yards from No. 2, which, despite the apparent contradiction of a fire underground, was a common and reasonably effective form of pit ventilation. Without constant firing the air flow fluctuated, but the system was also having to cope with unusually large areas of newly opened coal releasing huge volumes of gas into a flow made more complicated by the extent of the new workings.

The tragedy was compounded by uncertainty over the numbers who died. The song says 210 while some calculations put the death toll at 207, others at 212. The enquiry report gives the figure as 209 although the same document lists only 208, all adding to a confusion that is perhaps the most potent measure of the careless disregard that characterised much mining of this period. In the two years that followed, two more explosions at the colliery claimed the lives of six and twenty eight men.

The pit head buildings in this picture are very similar to contemporary drawings of the disaster, so these men could be at Blantyre No. 3. Blantyre was an extensive colliery with a central No. 1 shaft to the Ell and Main coals and three other shafts ranged around it with No. 4 about a mile away. Nos 2 and 3 shafts only worked the hard, gassy Splint coal which was in great demand for the furnaces of the iron industry.

The miner, sitting on the left of the picture on the previous page, is holding a pick shaft with a number of pick heads on it. He may have been taking them to, or collecting them from the blacksmiths. They were an essential part of any colliery and this group is typical of the men who made and maintained pit equipment. They also sharpened picks for the miners who had money deducted from their earnings to pay for the 'service'.

The Blantyre miners lived in Dixon's Rows, 340 houses in short blocks like this in Hall Street, one of four streets that made up the company village. Being tied houses, they were needed by the company and, after about six months the wives and children of men killed in the disaster were evicted. It was harsh, they faced destitution, but that was the tied house system and some women remarried to keep a roof over their heads!

Before it was partitioned and occupied, this block housed the first post reformation Catholic church in Blantyre. When a more permanent school cum church was built it reverted to being four single end houses.

A cup tie brought Blantyre Colliery to a standstill in March 1937. Hamilton Accies were playing Hearts and when the pit manager refused to adjust the men's shifts to let them go to the game, they just went anyway. A record crowd of 27,000 crammed into Douglas Park to see the Accies win 2-1. Football was a great miners' passion and this team Priory Rovers, is thought to have been formed from men working at the pit. The players in some of these early teams staked cash on the result of a game, the winners took all. Many great footballing men came from the Lanarkshire mining communities including Willie Waddell of Rangers, Jock Stein of Celtic and Sir Matt Busby of Manchester United.

Handball, played here by men at the Uddingston rehabilitation centre, was another popular game. It was like squash except that, instead of a racquet, the palm of the hand was used as a bat to hit a hard ball against the gable end of a two storeyed tenement.

Quoiting (pronounced 'kiteing') was another sport enjoyed in mining communities. The quoit was a heavy iron ring, flat on one side and rounded on the other, which the quoiter threw with great accuracy over eighteen yards at a steel peg in a three foot bed of clay. This group of Blantyre miners wore their political hearts on their quoiting sleeves; 'reds' are not their sporting colours – the team was made up of communist sympathisers. As with other miners' recreations, money changed hands on the results of quoiting matches although serious gamblers played pitch and toss.

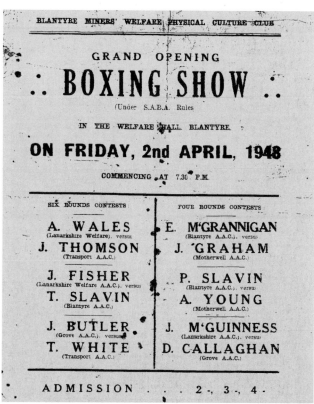

Boxing was a miners' sport too, as this handbill for the inaugural bill at the Blantyre Miners' Welfare Physical Culture Club shows.

Hamilton Palace was a showpiece pit sunk in the early 1880s by the Bent Colliery Co. Ltd to work coal leased from the Duke of Hamilton on the North Haugh of Hamilton Palace. The shafts, to the north of the Clyde on the Bothwell Haugh, initially went through alluvial deposits which had to be stabilised with a lining of timber and puddle clay. It was always a very wet pit and, before pumps were installed, water was gathered in a sump and lifted nightly in large tanks attached to the cages. The pit's prime coal, the Ell, was reached at a depth of 624 feet, although faulting divided the field into three portions and altered the levels by over 300 feet. Unusually for the time the pit was worked by a system of retreat mining in which the roadways were extended to the boundary and the coal cut back towards the pit bottom.

Wear and tear took its toll through the 1950s and a symptom of impending demise came in 1955 when a cage in No. 2 shaft jumped the guide rails at speed, collided with the other cage and jammed the two of them in the shaft. The pit closed in 1959.

In the years before the First World War nearly 1,400 people worked at the colliery and most lived in the isolated pit village of Bothwellhaugh. The houses were two storey brick tenements. There were some single ends, but most houses were room and kitchen and there were some two room and kitchens. In 1948 failing water supplies and inadequate drainage saw a sanitary closing order being imposed on the village by the Council, but the pit was dying and the village dying with it, and the problems were never mended. The last inhabitants had gone by 1965 and the site was incorporated into Strathclyde Park in the 1970s.

In 1915 the colliery owners were given permission to work the Ell seam under Hamilton Palace itself. The palace had long since ceased to be a residence for the Dukes of Hamilton who no doubt calculated that royalties earned from the coal would far outweigh the value of the building. Initially the company were not permitted to take coal from under the family mausoleum, but this restriction was later relaxed and it now sits tilted at an angle, a monument to the riches to be got from coal. The palace was one of the finest of Scotland's great houses and a loss to the country's heritage.

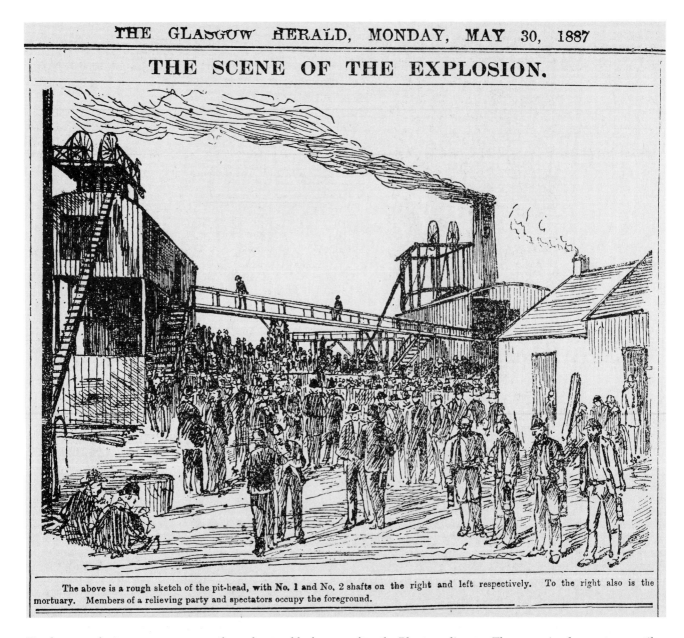

THE GLASGOW HERALD, MONDAY, MAY 30, 1887

THE SCENE OF THE EXPLOSION.

The above is a rough sketch of the pit-head, with No. 1 and No. 2 shafts on the right and left respectively. To the right also is the mortuary. Members of a relieving party and spectators occupy the foreground.

Firedamp explosions were not properly understood before, or after, the Blantyre disaster. They remained a mystery until the Saturday morning shift descended the Udston Coal Company's pit on 28th May 1887. The men had been working for over three hours when, at about 9 o'clock, a pillar of flame shot out of No. 1 shaft scorching the head frame timbers. At the same time the cage was blown out of No. 2 shaft carrying with it a seventeen year old boy who was smashed against the head frame and killed.

Sinking at Udston had begun in 1874 to work three seams, the upper Ell at about 780 feet, the Main 60 feet deeper and the Splint at just over 900 feet. It was ventilated by a 25 foot diameter extractor fan and, like Blantyre, was a naturally dry and dusty pit.

The first 'explorers' (as volunteer rescuers in those days were called) went into the Ell seam where all 40 men were found alive and only vaguely aware of the explosion. In the Main seam over 40 men had survived, but some had been overcome by the effects of whitedamp filtering up from below. It was clear that, as at Blantyre, the explosion had occurred in the Splint coal. Of the seventy men who had gone down that morning only two had survived. One was so badly injured that a special railway locomotive and van was laid on to rush him to Saint Rollox Station and Glasgow Royal Infirmary – there were no fast ambulances with sirens and flashing blue lights in those days.

Unauthorised shot firing was blamed for the accident, but the crucial finding at the inquiry was that the initial gas explosion had set off a more devastating coal dust explosion. The extent of the Blantyre tragedy could at last be explained as an initial explosion that had set off a chain reaction of many more. Within ten years the two worst disasters in Scotland's mining history had happened within a few miles of each other, but the Udston inquiry provided answers that would eventually improve pit safety.

A miner outside his thatch roofed cottage in the Hamilton area.

Earnock House was the home of Sir John Watson Bt, one of Lanarkshire's foremost coal owners. He was born in Kirkintilloch, the son of a stone mason from Fife who came west in 1814 and after a while went into the coal trade. Young John worked as a canal boatman for his father, leading and steering horse drawn coal scows through the night to Port Dundas. By the 1840s he was branching out on his own. He gained a lease at Wishaw and sunk a pit called the Victoria. He took the lease of another pit at Slamannan, sunk another pit, the Wellington, beside the Victoria and gained the lease of the new Parkhead colliery at Motherwell in 1858. He leased the 400 acre Motherwell coalfield in 1862, extended his interests near Slamannan and leased another area adjoining the Parkhead field where he sunk the Lady Emily pit. Turning his attentions to the Hamilton area he bought the estates of Neilsland in 1871 and Earnock in 1873. He began sinking Earnock Colliery four years later and in 1879 a small quantity of Ell coal was raised.

Earnock was a model colliery with the shafts arranged to protect man winding and allow for escape after an explosion. Electric light was installed in 1881 at the shaft bottoms, principal roadways and workings making it the first pit in Britain to be lit by electricity. The power house also supplied electricity to Earnock House. Telephone communication between the surface and pit bottom was also introduced adding to a list of wonders that attracted delegations of inquisitive civic and industry leaders from all over Scotland.

A new pit to work the Splint coal was sunk in 1891 and, by the First World War, Earnock was the biggest single unit in Lanarkshire employing nearly 1,500 people. By the Second it was nearing exhaustion and it closed in 1942.

John Watson bought the neighbouring Eddlewood estate in the 1880s, but did not gain access to Eddlewood Colliery until 1890, the same year that he turned the business into a limited company. The new company opened this reading room and recreation hall at Eddlewood in November 1892. It was some years ahead of its time and a precursor of the welfare institutes of the 1920s. The hall could hold 200 people and at the inaugural concert they were treated to a John Watson recitation of Burns' 'Cottar's Saturday Night'. A year later an almost identical facility was opened at Earnock with another opening concert and recitation. A bowling green was opened nearby in 1908.

The clean and dry appearance of Eddlewood village indicates significantly better water supply and drainage arrangements than at other mining communities.

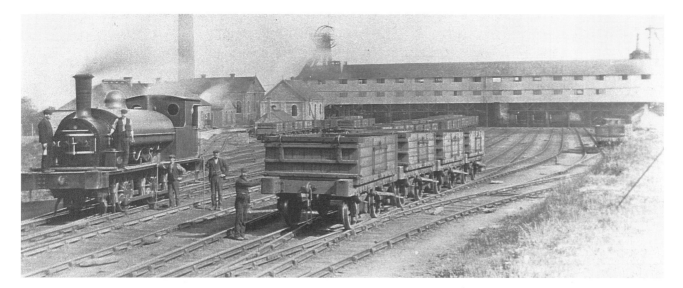

John Watson Ltd sunk a new pit on Neilsland estate, to the south east of Hamilton, in 1894. The eldest son of the family, also named John, cut the first sod of pit No. 1 and his younger brother Tom cut the first sod of No. 2. The symmetrical arrangement of pit head buildings and railway layout gave the colliery an unusually pleasing appearance. It started producing coal in 1895, the same year that the man who had once worked as a boatman became a baronet. Neilsland was worked in conjunction with Eddlewood and the two closed in 1932.

Hamilton gained a whole new district when the Cadzow Colliery village was built. It comprised about four hundred houses, some of which are seen here with washing poles and lines strung across the street. Cadzow was a very wet pit of three shafts sunk in the 1870s, it produced a high quality Ell coal which burned to the lowest ash content recorded by the Glasgow City Analyst. It was abandoned in 1937.

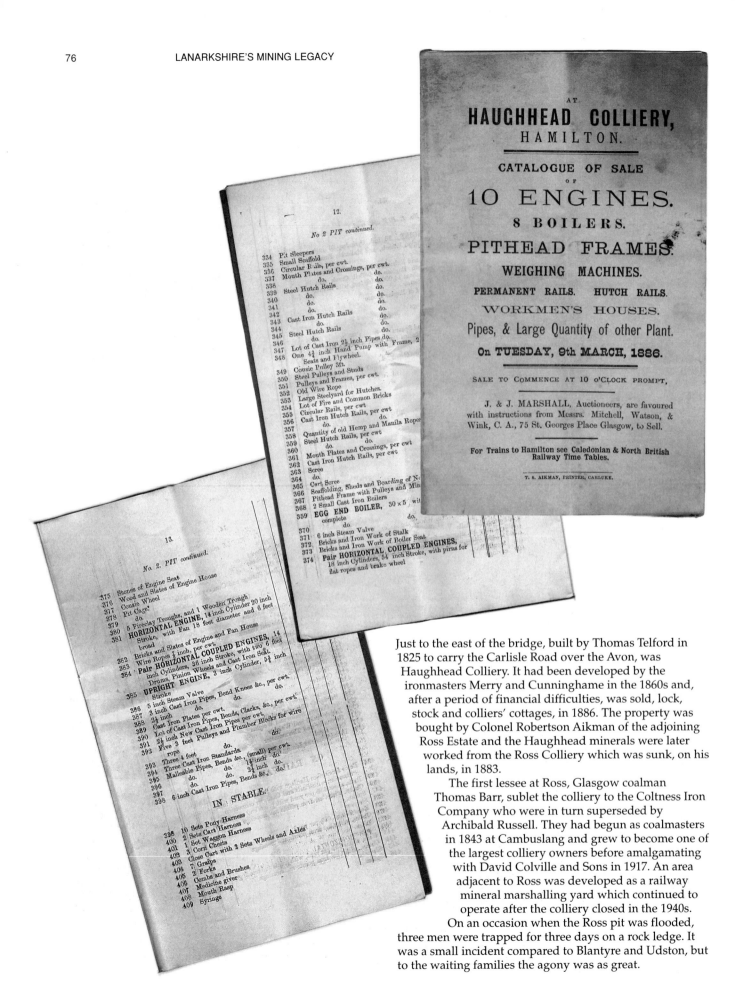

AT

HAUGHHEAD COLLIERY,
HAMILTON.

CATALOGUE OF SALE
OF

10 ENGINES.
8 BOILERS.
PITHEAD FRAMES.
WEIGHING MACHINES.
PERMANENT RAILS.   HUTCH RAILS.
WORKMEN'S HOUSES.
Pipes, & Large Quantity of other Plant.

On TUESDAY, 9th MARCH, 1886.

SALE TO COMMENCE AT 10 O'CLOCK PROMPT.

J. & J. MARSHALL, Auctioneers, are favoured
with instructions from Messrs. Mitchell, Watson, &
Wink, C. A., 75 St. Georges Place Glasgow, to Sell.

For Trains to Hamilton see Caledonian & North British
Railway Time Tables.

T. S. AIKMAN, PRINTER, CARLUKE.

12.

No 2 PIT continued.

334 Pit Sleepers
335 Small Scaffold
336 Circular Rails, per cwt.
337 Mouth Plates and Crossings, per cwt.
338   do.   do.
339 Steel Hutch Rails   do.
340   do.   do.
341   do.   do.
342 Cast Iron Hutch Rails   do.
343   do.   do.
344 Steel Hutch Rails   do.
345   do.   do.
346 Lot of Cast Iron 2½ inch Pipes do.
347 One 4¾ inch Hand Pump with Frame, 2
       Seats and Flywheel.
348 Cousie Pulley 3ft.
349 Steel Pulleys and Studs
350 Pulleys and Frames, per cwt.
351 Old Wire Rope
352 Large Steelyard for Hutches.
353 Lot of Fire and Common Bricks
354 Circular Rails, per cwt.
355 Cast Iron Hutch Rails, per cwt
356   do.   do.
357 Quantity of old Hemp and Manila Rope
358 Steel Hutch Rails, per cwt
359   do.   do.
360 Mouth Plates and Crossings, per cwt
361 Cast Iron Hutch Rails, per cwt
362 Scree
363   do.
364 Cart Scree
365 Scaffolding, Sheds and Boarding of N
366 Pithead Frame with Pulleys and Min
367 2 Small Cast Iron Boilers
368 EGG END BOILER, 30 × 5 wit
       complete   do.
369   do.   do.
370 6 inch Steam Valve
371 Bricks and Iron Work of Stalk
372 Bricks and Iron Work of Boiler Seat
373 Pair HORIZONTAL COUPLED ENGINES,
       18 inch Cylinders, 54 inch Stroke, with pirns for
       flat ropes and brake wheel

13.

No. 2. PIT continued.

375 Stones of Engine Seat
376 Wood and Slates of Engine House
377 Cousie Wheel
378 Pit Cage
379   do.
380 5 Fireclay Troughs, and 1 Wooden Trough
381 HORIZONTAL ENGINE, 14 inch Cylinder 20 inch
       Stroke, with Fan 18 feet diameter and 6 feet
       broad
382 Bricks and Slates of Engine and Fan House
383 Wire Ropes ¾ inch, per cwt.
384 Pair HORIZONTAL COUPLED ENGINES, 14
       inch Cylinders, 36 inch Stroke, with two 6 feet
       Drums, Pinion Wheels and Cast Iron Seat.
385 UPRIGHT ENGINE, 3 inch Cylinder, 5¾ inch
       Stroke
386 5 inch Steam Valve
387 3 inch Cast Iron Pipes, Bend Knees &c., per cwt.
388 2½ inch   do.   do.
389 Cast Iron Plates per cwt.
390 Lot of Cast Iron Pipes, Bends, Clacks, &c., per cwt.
391 2½ inch New Cast Iron Pipes per cwt
392 Five 3 feet Pulleys and Plumber Blocks for wire
       rope   do.
393 Three 4 feet
394 Three Cast Iron Standards.
395 Malleable Pipes, Bends &c.. (small) per cwt.
396   do.   do.   1¼ inch do.
397   do.   do.   2¼ inch do.
398 6 inch Cast Iron Pipes, Bends &c..

IN STABLE.

399 10 Sets Pony Harness
400 2 Sets Cart Harness
401 1 Set Waggon Harness
402 3 Corn Chests
403 Close Cart with 2 Sets Wheels and Axles
404 7 Graips
405 2 Forks
406 Combs and Brushes
407 Medicine giver
408 Mouth Rasp
409 Syringe

Just to the east of the bridge, built by Thomas Telford in
1825 to carry the Carlisle Road over the Avon, was
Haughhead Colliery. It had been developed by the
ironmasters Merry and Cunninghame in the 1860s and,
after a period of financial difficulties, was sold, lock,
stock and colliers' cottages, in 1886. The property was
bought by Colonel Robertson Aikman of the adjoining
Ross Estate and the Haughhead minerals were later
worked from the Ross Colliery which was sunk, on his
lands, in 1883.

The first lessee at Ross, Glasgow coalman
Thomas Barr, sublet the colliery to the Coltness Iron
Company who were in turn superseded by
Archibald Russell. They had begun as coalmasters
in 1843 at Cambuslang and grew to become one of
the largest colliery owners before amalgamating
with David Colville and Sons in 1917. An area
adjacent to Ross was developed as a railway
mineral marshalling yard which continued to
operate after the colliery closed in the 1940s.

On an occasion when the Ross pit was flooded,
three men were trapped for three days on a rock ledge. It
was a small incident compared to Blantyre and Udston, but
to the waiting families the agony was as great.

Ferniegair Colliery was opened in the 1850s but the owner got into financial difficulties with other ventures and Archibald Russell Ltd took it over. Under their (and David Colville's) ownership the colliery was expanded. Between the 1880s and 1920s the coal was extracted seam by seam from under Chatelherault, the splendid garden pavilion built to William Adam's design in 1732. The coal was apparently worth more than the estimated cost

of repairs to the decorative structure and fortunately (or perhaps thanks to the skill of the mining engineers) the cost did not include demolition. Continued expansion over the years created so many interconnecting old workings that latterly Ferniegair was a very difficult pit to ventilate. It struggled into Coal Board ownership but was immediately closed.

Double Row was part of the Allanton pit village which was next to William Barr and Sons' Allanton Colliery. Some of the pit head buildings can be seen on the extreme right of the picture which dates from 1910. The 'double' row was built back to back with another, hence the name. The muddy 'street' was typical of conditions that made cleanliness and hygiene in the tiny houses impossible.

Coal had been mined at Laigh (Low) Quarter for a few hundred years before the Duke of Hamilton sunk the first pit in 1815. The early colliers and their families lived in thatch roofed houses like these.

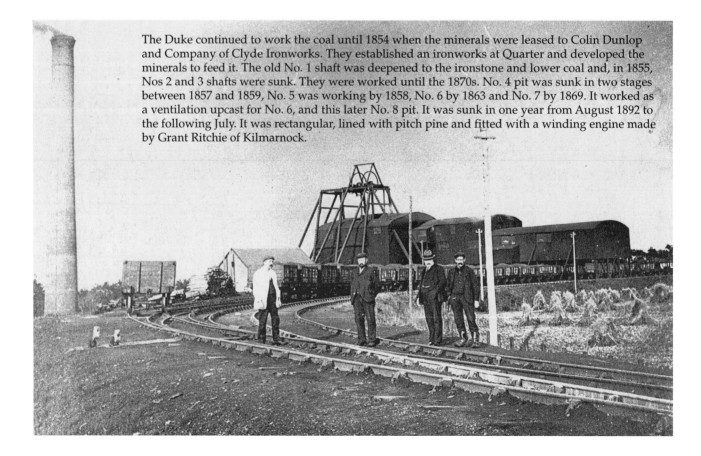

The Duke continued to work the coal until 1854 when the minerals were leased to Colin Dunlop and Company of Clyde Ironworks. They established an ironworks at Quarter and developed the minerals to feed it. The old No. 1 shaft was deepened to the ironstone and lower coal and, in 1855, Nos 2 and 3 shafts were sunk. They were worked until the 1870s. No. 4 pit was sunk in two stages between 1857 and 1859, No. 5 was working by 1858, No. 6 by 1863 and No. 7 by 1869. It worked as a ventilation upcast for No. 6, and this later No. 8 pit. It was sunk in one year from August 1892 to the following July. It was rectangular, lined with pitch pine and fitted with a winding engine made by Grant Ritchie of Kilmarnock.

Colin Dunlop & Co. also built a village of over 200 houses at Quarter with a pub as its only social diversion.

In an effort to provide a much needed alternative, Nina, Duchess of Hamilton built this institute. There was a meeting room, library, billiards, carpet bowls, baths and a skittle alley that doubled as a curling rink. The doors were opened in May 1910 and the formal opening followed in September. The architect presented the Duchess with a key, she unlocked the door and declared the institute open. She also threw the first bowl on the institute's new green. After closure in the 1950s, and a period of uncertainty, the building was rescued from dereliction and turned into a nursing home.

Many famous politicians and sporting heroes worked in Lanarkshire's collieries, but perhaps the county's most famous miner was the great entertainer Sir Harry Lauder. He started as a boy at Eddlewood pit head, before going underground to work as a trapper (operating a ventilation trap door) and then as a pony driver. He 'graduated' to the face, working in a number of pits in the Hamilton area and apparently also taking part in an underground concert with some fellow miners when they were trapped for some hours by a roof fall. While at Quarter No. 7 pit he made the classic career move for an ambitious young man by marrying the under-manager's daughter. He moved, not for the first time, to Allanton Colliery where a tolerant management gave him the freedom to develop his theatrical talents, before he made the final break from mining. During his stage career he never forgot his early life and campaigned to improve the lot of pit ponies which he had driven as a boy. His efforts were rewarded by legislation, in the Mines Industry Act of 1911, to protect ponies from casual cruelty.

When the National Coal Board took over in 1947 it faced a shortage of coal which old, exhausted pits could not supply. New pits were urgently needed, but time was needed to develop them and so the Board opened some small drift mines to meet the short term demand. They were also intended to keep miners, displaced from old pits, employed until the big new developments were ready. These mines were in proven fields although some went into areas that had been worked out and were quickly closed.

While none of the big new developments was in Lanarkshire, some of the short term mines were, one was Knowetop at Quarter, seen in these two pictures. It was opened in the early 1950s and was associated with other local mines, Beaton's Lodge and Avonbraes. They were the last mines in Scotland to use ponies for underground haulage. Knowetop was closed in 1966.

Avonbraes mine was driven into the steep sides of the Avon gorge on the site of an early mine called Avonbanks. It had been worked between 1824 and 1857 and its coal taken down the Avon valley by a mineral railway. While it was operating, a small mine at Quarter sent its coal across the valley to also use the mineral railway. The NCB worked the other way round, sending Avonbraes coal across to the Quarter side of the valley on this disused bridge.

It is hard, in these days of heat and light at the flick of an electric switch, to comprehend how important coal was to people and how enticing the prospect of getting it free. For centuries, people drove levels into outcropping seams in the sides of the Avon Valley to win coal, although here it appears to have been exposed in the bed of the river. These intrepid late nineteenth century folk are doing their best to ensure their supply for the coming winter.

Miners loved open air pursuits. Many tramped miles of countryside accompanied by lurcher dogs and some were expert hunters (poachers actually!) making a few bob from the sale of ill gotten hares, trout or vegetables. Some men preferred the altogether gentler pursuit of fleeing doos (flying pigeons!) and lofts like this, thought to have been in the Larkhall area, abounded in mining communities. Birds intended for races were trained over increasingly greater distances to fit them eventually for races from the Borders, England, the Channel Islands or France.

This picture was found in Larkhall and was taken by a Birkenshaw photographer, but it is not known if these men are from the Larkhall area or not (there is a Birkenshaw near Uddingston too!). They look like surface workers although one man has a 'tally' lamp on his cap and an early safety lamp in his hand. The Larkhall Fireclay Company, extracted household, manufacturing and steam coal, as well as fireclay from a Birkenshaw pit and the village was dominated by the fireclay industry with a sanitary engineering works and brick works.

Canderrigg Nos 4 and 5 was known locally as Broomfield pit. It was sunk by James Nimmo & Co.
Ltd in 1902 just to the south of Broomfield farm, hence the name. It worked the same field as
Canderrigg, or Canderside, Nos 2 and 3 pits, which were to the south east of Canderside Bridge.
Nos 6 and 7 Canderside mines were opened in 1939 and, with Broomfield, worked through to
nationalisation. The pits closed in 1954 and the mines ten years later. The seams were wet and
narrow. The roads too were very low and men had to be careful to push hutches with their hands
flat on the hutch or their fingers could be caught by the low roof.

After closure, the derelict and abandoned Broomfield was a sorry sight. The top picture shows the elevated hutch road from Canderside mine to the old washer, which can be seen in the lower picture and on the left of the picture of the working colliery on the previous page.

Broomfield was in the middle of the countryside and a mineral railway was laid to connect it to the Lesmahagow branch of the Caledonian Railway, between Canderside Toll and Birkenshaw. The picture was taken at the water tanks beside the minor road from Canderdikehead to Stonehouse. Industrial locomotives like this one built by George Inglis and Co. of Airdrie, were called pugs. The curious basket like cage on the funnel was a spark arrester, probably put there to avoid setting crops alight in the fields on either side of the line.

Between the minor road and the colliery, the pug line turned through 90° and crossed the Carlisle Road. In the 1900s this was probably not a problem, but a level crossing on the main Glasgow to London road no doubt caused much anguish in 1958, when the picture was taken. The pug

sedately trundling its empties across the road was built in 1902 by Scotland's foremost builder of industrial steam locomotives, Andrew Barclay of Kilmarnock. It spent its early years at John McAndrew & Company's Thankerton Colliery at Holytown, but was transferred to Canderrigg after nationalisation. It was scrapped in 1965, soon after the mine closed.

Dalserf Station, on the Caledonian Railway's Motherwell to Lesmahagow line, was originally known as Ayr Road Station. Just beyond it here is the head frame of Archibald Russell's Cornsilloch No. 4 pit. Had the photographer looked the other way along the railway, the view would have included the three headframes of the main colliery.

The horse collars proudly displayed by these 'Auldton drawers' only give a partial clue to the drawer's job. The men who actually used the ponies on underground haulage work were drivers. Those who drew full hutches out to the haulage roads and put empty hutches where the face men could fill them, were known as drawers and putters. Although such work was essential, the men doing it were known as on-cost workers because the cost of their labours was added on to the price of winning the coal. There were two Auldton collieries at the time the picture was taken – this is probably Brand and Company's pit at Ashgill which closed about 1914. The other 'Auldton', at Lesmahagow, closed in 1902. The NCB also operated an Auldton drift mine at Lesmahagow which closed in 1963.

A ridge of old red sandstone separates the coalfield to the south of Lesmahagow from the rest of Lanarkshire. It was famous for 'Lesmahagow' gas coal or cannel coal which people used as a source of light and was worked from shallow mines above the water table for so long that, by the time the railway arrived, it was exhausted. The new transport system made it profitable to sink shafts to the deeper levels and they had been working for about 75 years when the Coal Board took over. The pit head which can just be seen above the houses on the left here was one of the Poneil pits.

Bellfield pit was also known as Poneil Nos 3, 4 and 7. The colliery was to the east of the village on the south side of the railway from Lesmahagow and was operated by William Barr and Sons of Allanton Colliery until being abandoned in 1921.

The pit beyond the houses to the left centre of this picture was Auchlochan No. 6, one of eight Auchlochan pits sunk before 1900. No. 6 was 300 feet deep to the nine foot seam and worked as the ventilation upcast and pumping shaft for the neighbouring Nos 7 and 8 pits. The large house in front of the pit was once home to the pit manager and is now the manse.

Auchlochan Nos 9 and 10 were sunk by Caprington and Auchlochan Collieries Ltd around 1900 with twelve foot diameter brick lined shafts. They had to be deeper than the older pits to intersect with the dipping seams. When the company went into liquidation in the early 1930s the pits were taken over by William Dixon & Co. Ltd They de-watered the lower seams and carried out development work. At nationalisation Auchlochan was producing around 400 tons a day, but after reorganisation, which made the pit all-electric from coal face to the surface, its output went up to 550 tons. It also treated the other coal mined in the district. The colliery was closed progressively through the 1960s with Nos 6 and 7 shafts being shut down in 1961 and Nos 9 and 10 closing in 1968.

Bowing to the geological reality that the coalfield was an eastern extension of the Ayrshire field the NCB administered it as part of its East Ayrshire and later, Ayrshire areas. It enjoyed the same development status as much of Ayrshire. In the immediate Coalburn area production was expected to rise from just over 1,000 tons a day to 1,500. Auchlochan was the biggest unit and there were smaller units at Auchmeddans, Auldton, Westoun and Bankend. When the new drift mines were brought into production in the 1950s, the NCB's plans for the area were complete, but their expectation that the youngest miner would 'find a lifetime's employment' in local collieries turned out to be optimistic.

Across the road from Auchlochan Nos 9 and 10 were the two storeyed Glaikhead Rows.

The Coltness Iron Company started operations in Douglasdale in 1881 working a small mine near Ponfeigh. It was a sprat to catch a mackerel because they were soon in negotiations with the Earl of Home who agreed to the sinking of Douglas Colliery. The Earl's stringent conditions resulted in an unusually squat chimney, to preserve the scenic amenity of the valley of the Douglas Water. The development was begun in 1893 and completed in 1899. Railway companies apparently found the coal from the Douglas field ideal for express locomotives.

The pit, also known as Ponfeigh, became the NCB's parent colliery of the Douglas group and, scorning the original environmental concerns, the Board erected this new concrete winding tower and preparation plant at the colliery. After a fire in February 1967 the workforce was cut from 450 men to 200 and, with the output down to 250 tons a day, the pit was closed later that year.

Like many company villages Douglas Water was built in the same polychrome brickwork as the adjacent colliery, Powell Street here is typical of the old village. With the pit gone few of these old buildings remain but the isolated village is still dominated by coal. A huge opencast site on the hill above it would have the environmentally conscious old Earl birlin' in his grave!

The Coltness Iron Company liked to encourage people in its villages to participate in leisure activities, like the prize winning Douglas Colliery band here. Not that any encouragement was needed because band music was always popular in mining communities. Douglas Water people also competed successfully in local and national amateur dramatic competitions.

The new houses built at the top of Springhill Road, Douglas in 1926 had a good view to the other side of the valley where the Douglas Castle mine was sited at Douglas West. It was connected to the Rankin and Wilson mines. The Douglas Castle miners had to contend with one of Nature's crueller tricks; they had lovely deep seams to work in, but folding of the strata had thrown them almost vertical. Props set at the regulation 90° didn't so much hold up the roof as support the walls. Miners had to lay planks on the props to get them up to the next section of coal, prompting at least one miner from the Hamilton area to walk out complaining he'd never had to howk coal up a tree before!

Douglas Castle mine was opened in 1912 by Wilson's and Clyde Coal Co. The steep entry was driven in the nine foot coal to 1,000 feet from where a level mine was driven to intersect with the other seams. Douglas Castle itself has gone, demolished in 1937 before it was undermined, but one outward reminder of mining for the people of Douglas is a pond known as the Pike Hole. It fills a large hollow left after the surface subsided into the workings. Closure of the mine was announced in December 1958 with the Coal Board claiming it had been losing £100,000 a year for five years and the miners countering that 50 years of good house coal remained. A torchlight procession of 300 miners through the village failed to change the decision.

Glentaggart mine was opened in 1943 to win coal from badly faulted and disturbed strata. Fossilised mussels abounded in the area and on one occasion the miners found a fossilised tree. The mine produced a good house coal which was sold to coal merchants at the mine head and off the back of this lorry. Although the mine closed in 1969 the old surface buildings continued in use as a coal distribution depot, one that is apparently haunted. At around midnight, when only wild moorland creatures and the tumbling waters of the burn disturb the peace, a ghostly miner is said to appear. He walks across the yard from the engineering shop and disappears into the hillside where the old mine entrance is covered by a huge concrete slab!

Glentaggart and surrounding hills have long been tapped for their minerals and opencast working will dominate the area for some time to come. Nearby Glespin was always a mining community with a row of modern council houses along the main road replacing the old village of 'tarry rows'. They were roofed with tarred felt, hence the name. The last pit to operate in sight of Glespin was Kennox. Tragedy struck in May 1943 when three men, trapped by an inrush of water, were found three weeks later having succumbed to the effects of blackdamp. Kennox closed in 1972 leaving these surface buildings.

High in the lowering Lowther Hills the lead miners of Leadhills used a hammer and chisel to follow a vein of the lead sulphate ore, galena, through the dense greywacke (pronounced greywacky) rock of the Southern Uplands. In the gas free atmosphere they could work with naked lights, but faced the twin dangers of drowning in pockets of water or being crushed by rock falls – although they only propped rock where it looked unstable. A combination of bad hygiene and poor understanding of the dangers, however, meant that the main life shortening hazard for early miners and their families was probably lead poisoning. The lead mines were often unspectacular holes in the ground, but numerous small bings scattered around the village point to an extensive industry that has gone on for centuries.

The industry reached a peak in the early nineteenth century, but the price plummeted when cheap foreign lead was allowed into the country in the 1830s. Mining struggled through the next seventy years until the Caledonian Railway ran a branch line up from Elvanfoot in 1902, allowing these larger mines to operate. Mines and railway both closed in the 1930s although the New Glencrieff mine, across the Dumfriesshire border at Wanlockhead, worked for two brief years in the 1950s. The excellent Museum of Lead Mining there tells the story of the industry and includes a tour of an old mine.

The Duke of Hamilton's 70 room mansion, Dungavel House, on the Strathaven to Muirkirk road was leased by the NCB in 1950 for use as a residential school for young miners. They were to receive three months' preliminary training there before starting work underground. The first intake was in February 1951 and the school was formally opened on 30th June by the Earl of Balfour, the Scottish Divisional Chairman of the NCB. The school was divided into 'houses' named after castles, Edinburgh, Caerlaverock, Stirling and Saint Andrews.

Practical training for the boys was given at Kames Colliery at Muirkirk in Ayrshire, but before Robbie Robb could gain his certificate, there was a fatal explosion at the pit. Training at Kames was stopped, but to make sure the boys completed their courses the tennis courts were quickly transformed into replica underground workings. Entering through a hole in the wire fence the boys spent the day 'underground', listening to the world outside because, while it was dark enough, it was not soundproof. Undaunted, Robbie got his certificate.

The No. 15 Pit Cadder, near Bishopbriggs. Scene of the Great Disaster, whereby 22 men lost their lives on Sunday, Aug. 3rd 1913. Pub. by Walter Benton & Co Glasgow.

At about 8.00 pm on Sunday 3rd August 1913, fireman William Brown descended the Carron Company's, Cadder No. 15 pit, for a routine check. He found a raging fire and raised the alarm. Three of the twenty six men in the pit at the time escaped, but the others were trapped.

The pit, on the north side of the Forth and Clyde Canal between Lambhill and Bishopbriggs, had been sunk in the 1880s to just over 1,000 feet. It was worked by longwall advancing and the workings, sometimes dipping at an angle of 1 in 3, extended north under the River Kelvin into Stirlingshire.

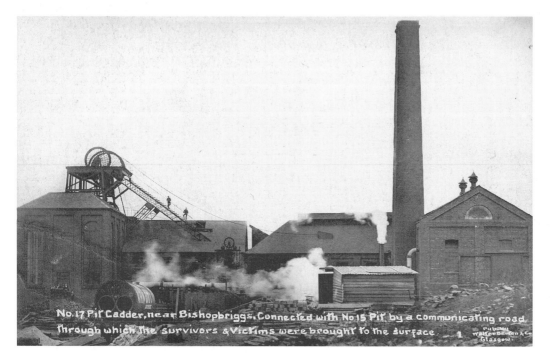

No. 17 Pit Cadder, near Bishopbriggs. Connected with No 15 Pit by a communicating road through which the survivors & victims were brought to the surface. Pub by Walter Benton & Co. Glasgow.

The rescue effort was concentrated on the neighbouring No. 17 pit which had been opened in the mid 1890s. It was about half a mile away and connected underground to No. 15.

By reversing the air flow the rescuers descended No. 17 with the downcast at their backs. A trap door led from the main communicating road into the workings, but gas forced the first two rescue parties back. The third rescue party reached five bodies, over six hours after the alarm was raised. One of the victims, a fireman named Charles Riley, could have saved himself, but had gone back to warn others.

Many of the rescuers lived in Mavis Valley, the adjacent mining village. They were not trained brigadesmen, but ordinary miners risking their own lives to help colleagues in trouble. The failure of the Lanarkshire Coal Masters Association to set up a rescue station, as required by the law of 1911, was severely criticised at the subsequent inquiry. The Fife & Clackmannan Association had set up a rescue team and they made what speed they could from Cowdenbeath. They were on unfamiliar roads and got lost in Kirkintilloch, but a friendly policeman directed them to the pit. Equipped with helmets and oxygen, they were able to penetrate deeper than the local men. They found one survivor amongst the bodies and by applying skills learned in training, brought him out alive.

As soon as the bodies had been recovered, the fire could be tackled. It was near the base of No. 15 shaft and the ventilation flow was reinstated to draw the fumes away from it. Hoses were laid down the shaft and groups of men, like these, went down in six hour shifts to pour millions of gallons of water on the blaze. Hampered by smoke, steam and the constant danger of a roof fall they worked round the clock, clearing debris as they went. After a few days they appeared to be winning the battle, but the fire flared up again. It burned for weeks and was eventually sealed behind brick walls. The pit was later re-opened, but closed in 1920.

This impressive procession of horse drawn hearses took seven of the victims from Mavis Valley, along the road beside the Forth and Clyde Canal to Cadder Cemetery. The village, which can be seen in the background, had to come to terms with the shared bereavement of family and neighbours, but, while the fire continued to burn, it also had to come to terms with unemployment. The Company offered work at other pits, but the money would not pay the rent at Mavis Valley and men were afraid of losing their houses.

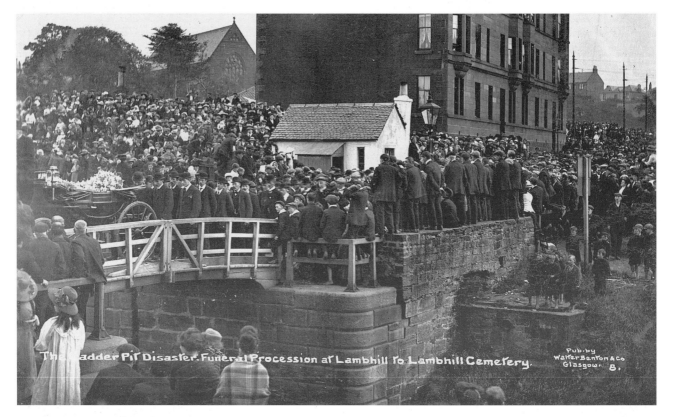

Most victims were buried in Saint Kentigern's cemetery at Lambhill and a memorial was later set up in their honour. Huge crowds, seen here at Lambhill canal bridge, came out at the funerals. Crowds with less savoury motives came to look at the ill fated pit the weekend following the disaster and extra trams had to be put on to the Lambhill terminus to cope with the numbers. The cause of the fire was never established. Cadder was not a gassy pit and a fire disaster was unexpected. The Company set up a trust fund under the Workmen's Compensation Act to provide for the widows and orphans, believed to be the first of its kind in Britain.

Wester Auchengeich, also known as the Lumloch pit, was originally sunk to a depth of 960 feet to work ironstone and was later reconstructed to work coal, very profitably! A toilet, installed at Wester Auchengeich above the deep, redundant ironstone shaft, solved the age old problem of providing facilities below the level of any sewer. It was a very 'convenient' arrangement until later development work, at the lower level, broke into the mess at the bottom of the shaft! Elsewhere, men used old workings to attend to calls of nature, some chalked a cross on a stone to mark the spot, while others used coal dust on their shovels to help 'wheech' the waste into the blackness!

Some of the Lumloch miners were bussed by the Coal Board from as far away as Blantyre and Larkhall. This, however, is the local service bus used by men from places like Hillhead, Kirkintilloch which, despite having lost its own coal industry, still had a large mining community.

Lumloch's connection with Auchengeich, three miles to the west, almost closed the pit prematurely. A spark in the Auchengeich workings in 1963 set off an explosion and fire which had to be sealed off with thirty foot thick walls of sandbags. Output at the two pits was brought to a standstill, but when it resumed, six days later, the worst effects were felt at Wester Auchengeich where 400 men were laid off. Months later the pit was brought back into production and remained in operation until 1968.

James Nimmo & Company's Auchengeich Colliery worked Kilsyth coking coal to produce a first class metallurgical coke, much in demand by the iron and steel industry. The pit was sunk in 1909 with a rectangular, timber lined, No. 1 shaft and a circular, brick lined No. 2 shaft, known as the 'round pit'.

The pit had an unhappy history. In 1931 an explosion in No. 2 pit, caused by unauthorised shot firing, killed six men and, on the day the enquiry opened, two more men died in a roof fall.

When the belting of an underground ventilation booster fan caught fire on 18th September 1959 it led to the worst disaster in a Scottish colliery for seventy years. The first group of men at the start of the day shift had descended on the bogie train to the working level when they encountered the fire. They made their way to the safety of the ventilation downcast but, before they could warn of the danger, the next trainload of men was already on its way down the 1 in 5 slope. They met the smoke being drawn up the roadway and signalled to be hauled back, but where the roadway levelled out, three hundred yards from safety, the train stopped. Forty seven men died, engulfed by the acrid smoke and gas. One man managed to get off the train and make his way to an alcove from where he was later carried unconscious, but alive.

The only way the fire could be extinguished was to flood the section of pit with water from the nearby burn. It was not pumped out again until the following June. At the subsequent enquiry the Coal Board was criticised for halting trials of self rescue equipment. These were restarted and self rescuers, which gave men about 30 minutes to get clear of the kind of situation encountered at Auchengeich, were first introduced to Scotland at the Kingshill pits in 1962.

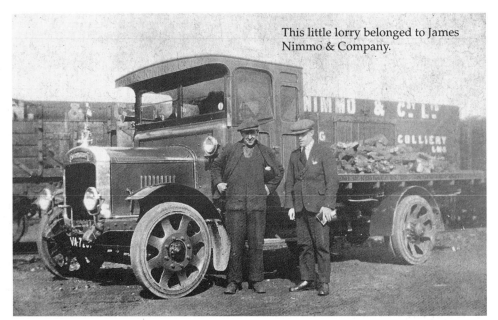

This little lorry belonged to James Nimmo & Company.

Above the shafts were the whorls, the huge pit head pulley wheels sometimes referred to as 'horrals'. They could be anything up to eighteen feet in diameter and this picture of one being hoisted on to the head frame at Auchengeich gives a good impression of their size. The grooved rim of the wheel was an open V section to allow free running of the rope and was four times the depth of the rope to guard against it jumping off the wheel.

Coal is the compressed, decayed remains of long dead trees that grew in primeval swampy lakes, fireclay is the bed of the lake. The clay was often found in sufficient thickness in coal mines to feed adjacent brickworks, but the huge deposits found in the Garnkirk to Glenboig area spawned a fireclay industry of its own. There were a number of large works, but in 1882, three men who had previously worked for rival concerns, came together to form the Glenboig Union Fireclay Company. They set up this, the largest brickworks in the world.

The fireclay seams of Glenboig were close to the surface and varied in thickness from 6 to 9 feet. It was not the soft, wet, pliable material used by potters; it was rock hard and had to be mined with explosives. Fireclay pits, like this at Garnqueen, were not gassy; miners were able to work with naked flame lamps and there were generally fewer serious accidents than in coal mines. The first for fifty years happened in 1909 at the Union Fire Clay Company's Star pit at Glenboig when a roof fall killed four men. The accident happened after a shot firing while the men were 'stooping out'.

Bedlay Colliery was sunk in undulating farmland at Annathill in 1905 by William Baird & Co. Ltd. It was a very gassy pit with thin seams, but despite these discomforts it was always regarded as a good pit to work in and its coking coal always wanted by the iron and steel industries. When the NCB took over there were three shafts; No. 1 went down 1224 feet, No. 2 was 738 feet deep and No. 3, 1166 feet. Coal, in 25 cwt. hutches, was wound in the first two and men and materials in No. 3.

Nationalisation was greeted in many ways, but one Bedlay miner marked the occasion by going to work in a suit, collar and tie – like any other civil servant! Plans to almost double the output to 1,200 tons a day followed the decision to build the Ravenscraig steel strip mill. The headgear over No. 1 shaft, in the centre here, was renewed and the frame from No. 3 shaft was moved to No. 2 (on the right). Winding was to be concentrated on No. 3 shaft and the new concrete winding tower, on the left, was erected over it. It was equipped with a four rope, electric friction winder and double decked cages. They could take 24 men on the top deck and 24 below, although these numbers were halved in an emergency. In case of trouble the cages could operate on a gravity basis by releasing water from counterweight tanks, but in one major power cut the electric pumps (that filled the tanks) and the ventilation were also out of action. The build up of gas turned an inconvenience into an emergency and one or two more than the regulation number of men jumped on the cages to escape!

As part of the reorganisation a new preparation plant, on the left here, was erected. It was capable of handling the output of both Bedlay and Auchengeich. Underground, the old continuous haulage system was replaced by battery locomotives hauling three ton mine cars on level roadways. The coal was cut by double ended ploughs that were drawn backwards and forwards along the face. A power plant was installed to generate electricity from pit gas. It was used to power pit head installations, heat bath water and prevent icing in the downcast shank when cold winter air was drawn down it. Ventilation systems were also reorganised to create an air flow of 200,000 cubic feet a minute. The development was completed in 1958.

Bedlay became a Mecca for railway enthusiasts who came to the colliery to see Scotland's last everyday working conventional steam locomotives. They moved waggons between the colliery and British Rail sidings off the old Monkland and Kirkintilloch Railway. Two days before the pit closed, pug No. 6, on the previous page, put on a show for the press and an appreciative throng of camera wielding admirers. They braved a clear frosty morning to witness a 'last day of operation' that nearly didn't happen because the points had frozen. Driver John Todd, encouraged by his shunter, Willie Bestel, gave them a dunt with the engine and, thus freed, she shunted into history. And came out again the following day to take a rake of empties to the BR sidings. She would have carried on the following day, but blew a fusible plug and so No. 17 was put in steam for the real last day, Friday December 11th 1981. She is seen here removing the last few waggons of coal from the washer, but, with her work complete, John Todd closed the regulator at 12.04. Bedlay's pugs, and Bedlay too, had reached the end of the line.

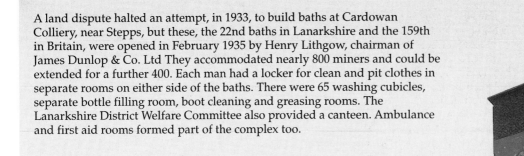

A land dispute halted an attempt, in 1933, to build baths at Cardowan Colliery, near Stepps, but these, the 22nd baths in Lanarkshire and the 159th in Britain, were opened in February 1935 by Henry Lithgow, chairman of James Dunlop & Co. Ltd They accommodated nearly 800 miners and could be extended for a further 400. Each man had a locker for clean and pit clothes in separate rooms on either side of the baths. There were 65 washing cubicles, separate bottle filling room, boot cleaning and greasing rooms. The Lanarkshire District Welfare Committee also provided a canteen. Ambulance and first aid rooms formed part of the complex too.

Cardowan was beside the old Garnkirk and Glasgow railway. It was sunk in the late 1920s by James Dunlop and Co. to work the Meiklehill Main and Kilsyth Coking Coal. Before it was complete it revealed its gassy nature when three pit sinkers were killed in an explosion in No. 2 shaft. There were sufficient volumes of gas in the pit to fire the boilers for the steam driven winding engines.

As part of their training, staff from the Uddingston rehabilitation centre had to go on site visits. These young women were pictured at Cardowan before it was redeveloped in the 1950s.

Despite being a high production pit, redevelopment was not a foregone conclusion. The large Comedie Fault, one and a half miles to the south of the pit dropped the working seams 720 feet below the level being worked from Cardowan and over 2,000 feet below the surface. Reserves were estimated at more than 25 million tons, but the NCB had to choose between the high cost of sinking a new pit in the Baillieston area or driving underground mines from the Cardowan workings. They decided to develop Cardowan and work started in the late 1950s. These existing shafts were relegated to ventilation and ancillary winding and a new circular shaft with four cages and electric winders was sunk. A new preparation plant was also installed.

Level roadways were driven for battery locomotives to haul mine cars, like these in the car hall on the surface. As at Bedlay, gas was a major problem and some sections were worked with pneumatic picks. A drainage plant was installed to pipe about 50 million cubic feet of methane a year, to Glasgow's Provan Gas Works. The gas, which equated to about one day's supply for the city, had double the heating value of town gas and the scheme paid for itself within a year. Gas was also piped to Buchanan's whisky bottling plant at Stepps.

Despite early signs of success, when the new underground mines hit a rich pocket of Main coal before they were completed, Cardowan failed to meet its increased target. It was nearly closed in 1969, but was reprieved and continued to operate through the 1970s. It was the only deep pit left in Lanarkshire when Bedlay closed

In January 1982, a violent explosion injured forty one men. Mercifully the coal dust failed to ignite, so the effect of the blast was less than it could have been. The explosion seemed to erode confidence in the pit and there was little resistance when closure was announced in May 1983. Union attempts to block transfers of men to other pits brought instant closure, which was accepted in a ballot. A few months later, the industry erupted in the last great national strike, but Lanarkshire had no pits left to fight for.

This great steam winding engine from the old No. 3 shaft, built by Murray and Paterson of Coatbridge, was dismantled and set up at Summerlee Heritage Park in Coatbridge. A replica mine and rebuilt miners' rows at Summerlee also recreate the mining experience and help to remind visitors that today's comforts have been won by yesterday's hardship and toil!

ACKNOWLEDGEMENTS

It would be an understatement to say that I have struggled to find material for this book and so I am very grateful to the many people from former mining communities who helped me, with anecdote and pictures, to compile this story; Willie Brown, Angus 'Gus' MacArthur, James 'Brancher' Fingland, Matt Clelland, 'Big Ned' Rafferty, George 'The Lum' Gardiner, Robert 'Robbie' Robb, Jim Fleming, Eddie McLaughlin, James 'Corny' Cornfield, David Pillans, Ramsay Armstrong, Jim Beveridge, Alex Lithgow, Mrs M. McMahon, Mrs A.E. McKechnie, Netta Devlin, Lt.Col. Sir John Inglefield-Watson Bt, the Rev. Brian Cross, Sheila Paul, Jess Meek, Charlie Thomson, Mr Semple of Blantyre and William Eaton. I must also thank the volunteers at the Scottish Mining Museum, especially George Gillespie, George Archibald, Campbell Drysdale and Andrew Shaw for their help and unfailing good humour. Private collectors too helped by supplying pictures and I must thank, Terry Harrison, Andy Stuart, Marjeorie Mekie and Ken Liddell.

I am also grateful to the custodians of public collections for their considerable help.

u – upper picture; m – middle picture; l – lower picture

The following photographs are reproduced by courtesy of;
Crown Copyright: Royal Commission on the Ancient and Historical Monuments of Scotland: 24(u); 108(u); 109(u); 110/111.
Scottish Mining Museum, Newtongrange: 12(u); 14/15; 28(u&l); 29(l);35(u); 36/37; 41; 42(l); 43(l); 44/45; 46(l); 47(u); 53(l); 54/55; 61; 62/63; 70(l); 92(u); 101(u).
North Lanarkshire Museum and Heritage Services: 18(u&l); 23 (u); 25(u); 26(u&l); 27(u); 37(u); 42(u&l); 43(u); 70(u); 104(l).
Leisure Services, South Lanarkshire Council: 58; 59(u); 75(u); 77(u); 78(l); 82(l).
William Patrick Library, Kirkintilloch: front cover; 100(u); 101(l); 102(l); 103; 105(l); 106; 107.
The Mitchell Library, Glasgow City Libraries and Archives: 16(l); 17(u&l); 72.
Springburn Museum: 6(u&l); 7(u).
David Livingstone Centre, Blantyre: 66; 67(u); 73(u).

A few anonymously published pictures appear in this book; the publishers will be pleased to entertain acknowledgements in these cases for future editions.

'Old Pals', miners and pony about 1900, believed to be at Auldton pit, Ashgill.